Lecture Notes of the Institute
for Computer Sciences, Social Informatics
and Telecommunications Engineering   60

Federico Alvarez   Cristina Costa (Eds.)

User Centric Media

Second International ICST Conference
UCMedia 2010
Palma de Mallorca, Spain, September 1-3, 2010
Revised Selected Papers

 Springer

Volume Editors

Federico Alvarez
Universidad Politécnica de Madrid, E.T.S.
Ingenieros de Telecomunicacíon
Avenida Complutense 30
28040 Madrid, Spain
E-mail: federico.alvarez@upm.es

Cristina Costa
CREATE-NET
Via alla Cascata 56/D
38123 Povo, Trento, Italy
E-mail: cristina.costa@create-net.org

ISSN 1867-8211
ISBN 978-3-642-35144-0
DOI 10.1007/978-3-642-35145-7
Springer Heidelberg Dordrecht London New York

e-ISSN 1867-822X
e-ISBN 978-3-642-35145-7

Library of Congress Control Number: 2012952040

CR Subject Classification (1998): H.5.1-3, H.3.1, H.3.3-4, H.4, H.2.4, H.2.8

Typesetting: Camera-ready by author, data conversion by Scientific Publishing Services, Chennai, India

Printed on acid-free paper

Springer is part of Springer Science+Business Media (www.springer.com)

Preface

UCMedia 2010 was the Second International ICST Conference on User-Centric Media. The conference was initiated in 2009 in Venice, Italy, targeting to provide a unique international forum for researchers in the field of user-centric multimedia technologies. In 2010 the conference was held in Palma, Majorca (Spain), an extraordinarily beautiful place in the Mediterranean, with crystal-clear waters and ideal weather.

User-centric media is one of the most relevant changes in the way the users consume, interact, and behave on the Internet in the last 5 years. The explosion of user-generated contents and social networks has made the user-centric media technologies one of the pillars of the future "Media Internet." In addition to the technical challenges, business models for sharing, exchanging, delivering, and experiencing multimedia services efficiently need to be addressed.

The aim of the Second International ICST Conference on User-Centric Media, UCMEDIA 2010, was to enhance the understanding of recent and anticipated advances in user-centric media creation, discovery, distribution, and consumption in the Future Internet, and their applications to entertainment, education, information, and the arts. UCMedia 2010 was a forum to present and discuss contributions from different domains, related to technology, business, the creative process, and user-based studies.

The UCMedia 2010 conference addressed these issues with technical sessions focusing on personalized access to multimedia content solutions, search and retrieval of networked multimedia content, multimedia and user experience, video quality perception and user quality of experience, user-generated content, content distribution and content summarization. In addition, there was a workshop on the first day of the conference: the 4th InterMedia Open Forum.

These proceedings are divided into eight different sections covering the above-mentioned topics of the conference. A total of 19 selected papers can be found in this book with a balanced covering of topics.

We would like to thank all the volunteers who shared their talent, dedication, and time for the conference organization and support as well as all our technical and financial sponsors. UCMedia 2010 was technically sponsored by ACM and the ACM Special Interest Group on Computer Human interaction. We would like to also thank our other sponsors: ICST, Create-Net, nextMEDIA, and the media partners Opinno and the MIT *Technology Review*. We would like to thank the Universitat de les Illes Balears and all the volunteers in the local organization who participated and made this conference possible.

We would especially like to thank our Local Organizing Chair, Toni Bibiloni, the members of our Steering Board, Imrich Chlamtac and Petros Daras, the Sponsorship Chair, David Jimenez, the Workshops Chairs, Francesco Calabrese and Mauro Martino, and the Technical Program Committee members. We would like to give a special thank you to the conference co-ordinator Mona Hezso, who did a tremendous job for the conference organization.

It was our pleasure to have had two keynotes of excellent quality as part of the conference program. We would like to thank Leonardo Chiarigione and Theodore Zahariadis.

We would also like to thank the participants who attended the conference during September 1–3, 2010.

Federico Alvarez
Cristina Costa

Organizing Committee

General Chair

Federico Alvarez   University Politecnica de Madrid, Spain

Program Chair

Cristina Costa   Create-Net, Italy

Local Arrangements Chair

Tony Bibiloni   Universitat de les Illes Balears, Espain

Sponsorship Chair

David Jimenez   University Politecnica de Madrid, Spain

Workshops Chairs

Francesco Calabrese   Senseable City Lab, MIT, USA
Mauro Martino   Senseable City Lab, MIT, USA

Technical Program Committee

Amar Aggoun	Brunel University, UK
Andrea Sanna	Politecnico di Torino, Italy
Antonio Camurri	University of Genoa, Italy
Antonio Servetti	Politecnico di Torino, Italy
Audrius Jurgelionis	University of Genoa, Italy
Dimitrios Tzovaras	ITI, CERTH, Greece
Dimitris Protopsaltou	Miralab - University of Geneva, Switzerland
Edison Spina	PUSP
Francesco Calabrese	MIT
George Papagiannakis	Miralab - University of Geneva, Switzerland
Helen C. Leligou	Technological Educational Institute of Chalkis, Greece
Jan Bouwen	Alcatel-Lucent
Jesus Vegas	University of Valladolid, Spain
Margarita Anastassova	CEA

Table of Contents

Section 4: Video Quality Perception and User Quality of Experience

Section 5: User Generated Content

Section 6: Content Distribution

Section 7: Content Summarisation

Section 8: Intermedia Open Forum: IMOF 2010 Workshop

A Tunable K-Hop Mobility-Based Outsourcing Replication Model for Optimizing End-to-End Reliability in MP2P Systems Using Community-Oriented Neighboring Feedback

Constandinos X. Mavromoustakis

Department of Computer Science, University of Nicosia
46 Makedonitissas Avenue, P.O. Box 24005, 1700 Nicosia, Cyprus
mavromoustakis.c@unic.ac.cy

Abstract. This work proposes a scheme which takes into account the k-hop mobility-based outsourcing strategy where the mobile devices are using a sequential scheme for caching requested high ranked resources onto neighboring nodes in the k-hop path in order to be available during a request. The scheme takes into consideration the relay epoch and the mobility aspects of each node in the k-hop path in order to disseminate effectively and within a specified duration any requested file chunks. The combined community oriented model enables the involved nodes in the path to contribute into the diffusion process pathetically according to the k-hop replication diffusion scenario using a feedback oriented mechanism which increases the multicasting diffusion throughput response significantly as simulation results show.

Keywords: mobility and adaptation methodology, MP2P systems, caching and outsourcing data, reliability technique, community-oriented neighboring feedback.

1   Introduction

The present work is motivated by the design of protocols in Mobile Peer-to-Peer (MP2P) networks that seek for nodes in order to assign to them specific roles such as forwarding capability as mediator nodes in cooperative caching, as well as for message ferrying nodes in Delay Tolerant Networks [1], rebroadcasting nodes in vehicular networks [2] etc.c. Peers are prone to failures and aggravate the end-to-end performance whereas short connections times or sudden disconnections (with chained unpredictable disconnections due to range and battery failures) reduce the overall resource availability of the MP2P system. The present work proposes a new technique called as k-hop mobility-based cache replication strategy where the mobile devices are using a sequential scheme for caching requested high ranked resources onto other neighboring nodes in the k-hop path in order to be available during a request. The scheme takes into consideration the relay epoch and the mobility aspects of each node in the k-hop path in order to disseminate effectively and within a specified duration

F. Alvarez and C. Costa (Eds.): UCMEDIA 2010, LNICST 60, pp. 1–9, 2012.

any requested packets. The proposed scheme utilizes the systems resources and comprises of a new model for disseminating information in a MP2P system. The proposed model enables greater stability in the offered resource availability on-the-go, and end-to-end reliability, whereas it increases the throughput of the system by increasing the throughput per source-destination pair scale with the number of nodes n. The proposed model enables the involved nodes in the path to contribute into the diffusion process pathetically according to the k-hop dissemination scenario using structured topologies and increases the multicasting diffusion throughput response significantly as simulation results show.

2   Related Work

Determination of the appropriate values of fundamental device parameters (e.g., the optimal caching parameter in accordance with other tuned measures) is a difficult task. When a mobile node makes an explicit request for a resource, and the whole network is flooded with a single query, as is the case with many mobile ad-hoc route discovery algorithms [3, 4] the scheme for information dissemination should be efficient enough, to enable recipients of the information to receive the requested info, and at the same to time reduce in the least possible degree the redundant duplications. Similar to file discovery by query flooding in P2P networks, like Gnutella, and unlike the proposed scheme in [5] which enables efficient and consistent access to data without redundant message generated communication overhead, the proposed scheme considers the flooding occasion which was found [6, 7 ,8] that reduces dramatically the end-to-end performance of the network.

Different caching approaches used, for enabling the requested data content to be available and discoverable [10, 11] at any time such that content can be discovered in a peer-to-peer manner. Additionally if all nodes are moving using a pattern or a path (as in vehicular networks) the requested data should be available within a specified interval and the selective or unselective dissemination process should forward the requested packets to destination [1, 2 10, 11] in a bounded time delay since devices are moving and the topology changes in time. Thus cooperative caching can speedup the streaming process, since the processing and delivery of multimedia content are not independent. Thus, cooperative caching results in lower latency, energy dissipation and packet loss [12].

The asymmetry in nodes' resources which significantly affects the stability of the sharing process (hosting many capacity and energy constraints) should be balanced using a scheme fulfilling all these requirements. A previous effort on a part of this problem is studied in [13] where the "repopulation" process is applied for facing node failures. The proposed model uses decentralized control in the manipulation of the requested resources and the communication between the peers in the network (sequence aspect). This applies in particular to the fact that no node has central control over the other. In this respect, communication between peers takes place directly. The outsourcing concept for the k-hop scheme is proposed in the next section which attempts to fill the trade-offs between user's mobility, reliable file sharing and limited throughput in exchanging delay sensitive data streams in mobile peer to peer environments. Examination through simulation is performed for the offered reliability by the collaborative replication k-hop scheme showing the increase in the grade of robustness in sharing resources among mobile peers.

3   K-Hop Cooperation Scheme and Mobility Model in Clustered Mobile Peer-to-Peer Devices

In this work in order to avoid any redundant transmissions and retransmissions we propose the clustered-based mobility configuration scenario which is set in figure 1 consisting of the single lane approach and multiple lanes approach. Clusters enable the connectivity between nodes and the local (within a cluster) control of a specified area. On the contrary with [8] in this work a different mobility scenario is examined where the node controlled area is not specified (unless a cluster cannot be formed) - like the Landscape in [8, 10]. The mobility scenario is based on a real time following a probabilistic path like in the real vehicular pathways.

Cluster network formation works as follows: each cluster is responsible to host newly added nodes and measures (Cluster Head (CH) responsibility) whether these nodes can host new file chunks. If the new node entered the cluster i has available remaining capacity greater than the existing CH, then this node becomes a CH and maintains the connectivity. The selected CH has as a responsibility to drive the transfers (between nodes) and restrict transfers which may be inadequate in terms of resources (coverage, connectivity, lack of relay nodes etc). In our model we have enabled the *probation slot* parameter which basically evaluates the time the node which has entered the cluster and after T_s *probation slot* the node can be either CH candidate or a member of a cluster to share resources. Connectivity can change network state also when a user moves to a different location and data need to be delivered from a source user to another then the relay mechanism can be interrupted and user experiences data losses.

In order to enable recoverability a replication scheme is designed using the k-hop replication algorithm as follows: each node creates, using the common look-up table for the requests, a ranking-based criteria selection of the requests of any files and/or packets by the nearby nodes. Since each node-based on the mobility scenario examined in the next section- will remain for a specified amount of time in the same path then the node i, which gets the requests forward copies of the packets to k-nodes in the path in the two directions (as in figure 1). Then each node which receives the requests do the same ranking procedure for their requests and forward the requested file chunks to k-nodes in the path in both traversing directions. The ranking process for the *i-resource* of the *N-node* ($Rank(i_N)$) that is set in the cluster C_i. takes place only in the formed cluster C. In this way there is a spine-based tree of replicated objects consisting of several nodes in the clustered path, while nodes with high ranked requests for specified file chunks continually create replicas for other nodes. This model enables high resource availability while maintaining the connectivity among peers that are requesting common resources.

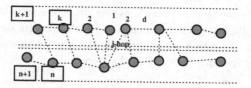

Fig. 1. Inter-cluster outsourcing of file chunks in order to be available according to ranking requests. j-hop comparisons with j-1 neighboring nodes are taking place for avoiding saturation of the replication scenario.

The tree of replicated objects is created-as in [10], considering the mobility model and the likelihood in accessing the certain path using social-model interactions, the update rate of the requests, the cost of the n-hop replications as well as the replay costs between m-different relay regions. Considering that the above scenario is used in real-time like in a vehicular raw-lane network, where requests of the j-hop may have a different direction, then it stands that for $Rank(i_N)$:

$$Min[Rank(i_N)]\forall N \notin C_i \qquad (1.0)$$

is minimized for the node that the resource was downloaded at least once or when the distance d is over a certain threshold D_{thress} from the k-hop peer- which means that the requested resource(s) set on this node has been redirected to any other path. Equation 1.0 sets the rank of the node containing the requested resource to minimum for the nodes that are not member of the cluster where the resource was requested iff d is over a certain threshold D_{thress}. If the D_{thress} becomes big enough then the resource is isolated and it no longer belongs to the C_i. This enables the prevention of huge duplicated information delivery, whereas it considers the nodes which are located far from source node and to maintain only the j-hops duplications-after the performed comparisons- avoiding redundant transmissions.

Considering the k-hop scenario of figure 1, the evaluated duration of the requested file chunks is evaluated as follows:

$$C_d = k \cdot E_i \qquad (1.1)$$

where C is the caching duration that is allowed for node i and E_i is the relay epoch according to the number of hops permitted. Therefore it stands that the greater the number of hops, then the greater the time duration that is allowed to be achieved. The delay epoch duration is modelled according to equation 1.5, taking into account the hop-count path, ping delays and the total delays from the end-to-end perspective.

3.1   Using Community Oriented Relay Regions

When streaming in a region and the packets sent are considered as prioritized, then these packets have a bounded time delay τ to reach any specified destination. The streaming parameter is based on the number of hops from a source to a destination and on the relay region and enclosure graph [9]. The relay region of a certain transmitter–relay node pair (u,w) identifies the set of points in the plane (node locations) for which communication through the relay node is more reliable than direct communication. Formally a *Relay region is considered to be as in [9]:*

$$RR_{u \to w} = \{(x, y) \in \Re^2 : P_{u \to w \to (x,y)} > P_{u \to (x,y)}\}. \tag{1.2}$$

where $P_{u \to w \to (x,y)}$ is the probability for a certain node u to transfer the file chunks from a source node x to destination node y via the w based on the connectivity and the social interactions described in the next section. Thus in an end-to-end path $\forall u \in P_n$ the minimized ping delays between the nodes in the end-to-end path the minimized evaluated delay is according to the:

$$d_p = Min \sum_{i=1}^{n} D_i \tag{1.3}$$

where D_i is the delay from a node i to node j, and d_p is the end-to-end available path. Therefore the delay epoch $E_{i(t)}$ of each node is defined as a function of the number of created replicas on the j-hosts as follows:

$$E_{i(t)} = d_{r_{i \to j}} \cdot {r_{i \to j}} \Big/ {Total\_d_{r_{i \to j}}} \tag{1.4}$$

where D is the delay via the ping assigned durations, $r_{i \to j}$ is the number of replicas form node i to j in the j-hop path and $Total\_d_{r_{i \to j}}$ is the total duration that all the requested replicas can be downloaded from the j-hop path.

3.2   Considering Mobility Models for Enabling Minimum Latency Outsourcing for Collaborative Neighboring Caching

Assume that we consider a Brownian-like motion with semi-random fields of characterization. In Brownian-like motion, the position of a node at a given time step depends (in a certain probabilistic way) on the node position at the previous step. In particular, no explicit modeling of movement direction and velocity is used in this model. An example of Brownian-like motion is the model used in [15]. Mobility is modeled using three parameters: p_{stat}, p_{move} and m. The first parameter p_{stat}, represents the probability that a node remains stationary for the entire simulation time. Parameter p_{move} is the probability that a node moves at a given time step. Parameter m models, to some extent, velocity: if a node is moving at step i, its position at step i + 1 is chosen uniformly at random in the square or side 2m centered at the current node position. Since in our case study we have examined the scenario of the movements of the nodes where nodes are moving in real-time pathways (roads,streets, corridors et.c.), it is important to denote that the probabilistic Brownian two-dimensional motion [10] can be an emulation of the real-time movements of the users in a certain pathway.

Definition 1.3 (Likelihood of the multiple selection connectivity path): The multiple selection connectivity path of a certain transmitter–relay node pair *(u,w)* traversing the formed *n* paths/clusters for time t, can be maintained within this time t if the nodes follow the same trajectory movements with likelihood as follows:

$$C_{u \to w} = \{(x, y, u, w) \in \Re^2 : P_{C_1 \in (u,x,y,w)} > P_{C_2 \in (u,x,y,w)} \forall u, w \in C_n\}. \tag{2}$$

Thus in an end-to-end path $\forall u \in P_n$, the likelihood of following the path P_1 instead of P_2 for node u and w in the cluster C_1 is following the p_{move} of the node which is the probability that a node moves at a given time step into a certain direction using the unit vector m.

3.2.1 Intercommunity Streaming and Download Frequency of the File Chunks

The metrics modeled are community-oriented and are considering the number of created clusters $C_N(t)$ in a specified Relay region of a certain transmitter–and a number of receivers (1, N] under the relay node pair (u,w) -as a modified definition of [9]- as follows the:

$$C_N(t) = \frac{2|h_N(t)|}{|I_{C(N)}(t)| \cdot (|I_{C(N)}(t)| - 1)}, \text{ iff } P_{u \to w \to (x,y)} > W_N(t) \tag{3.1}$$

where W is the Community streaming factor and is defined as the number of existing communities in the intercluster communicational links at a given time instant. The $h_N(t)$ is the number of hops in the existing clusters and the $I_{C(N)}(t)$ is the number of interconnected nodes N in the cluster $C_N(t)$.

A community is defined as a dense sub-graph where the number of intracommunity edges is larger than the number of intercommunity edges [9]. W can be defined according to the download frequency of the file chunks in the intercommunity as follows:

$$W_N(t) = \frac{DldRate \cdot \# sharingChunks}{Total \# dlds(t) \cdot \# inactiveChunks} \tag{3.2}$$

where in (1.4) the download rate is considered in contrast with the number of chunks being shared in a specified instant time *t*.

3.2.2 Neighboring Feedback for File Chunk Indices

Neighbor $N_j(t)$ at a certain instant of time, informs the *k*-neighbor receivers for the existence of the file chunk onto this node, according to the following:

$$R_{j \to 1..k} = \{\lim_{N \to K} C_{n(t)} \in W_N(t) : h_N(t) > \frac{N(N-1)}{2}\} \tag{3.3}$$

This means that for a specified amount of time the neighbors collaboratively can provide any node which exists in the Community with a streaming factor W with the feedback and can be locally informed about any requested file chunk at the specified time t. Provided that all the assumptions were made under the k-hop replication scheme described in the previous section in order to enable reliable file chunks sharing among mobile peers using a neighboring cluster-based feedback outsourcing.

4   Performance Analysis through Simulation and Discussion

The implementation-simulation of the proposed scenario was performed in C/Objective programming language libraries were used as in [8] and as a routing approach we have used a combination of the Zone Routing Protocol (ZRP) [16] with the Cluster-based Routing Protocol (CRP). Figure 2 shows the number of hops with the delay/latency for the nodes that requested replicas were created. This figure shows that in the case of not having a feedback response, the number of hops that replicas were created is significantly increased compared with the number of replicas created

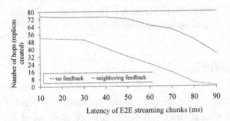

Fig. 2. Number of hops with the delay/latency for the nodes that requested replicas were created

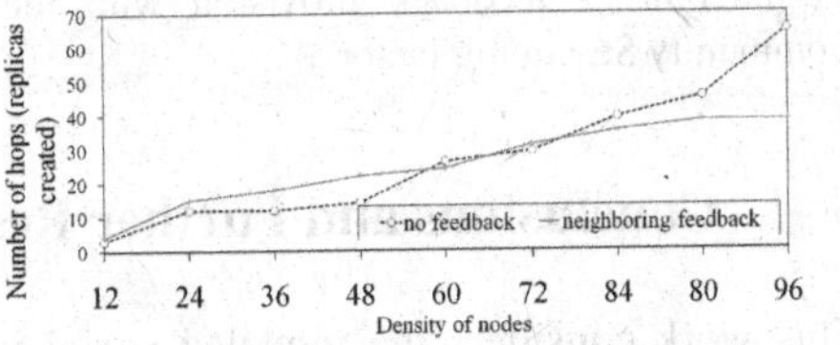

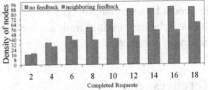

Fig. 3. Number of hops with the density of the nodes in the cooperation scenario

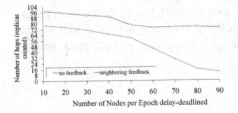

Fig. 4. Number of hops with the density of the nodes per epoch delay deadline used in the cooperation scenario

Fig. 5. Density of nodes with the completed requests

when feedback takes place. Additionally the latency in the first case is significantly higher and as shown reduces the throughput response of the system significantly. Figure 3 shows the number of hops with the density of the nodes in the cooperation scenario whereas figure 4 shows the number of hops with the density of the nodes per epoch delay deadline used in the cooperation scenario. In figure 5 the density of nodes with the completed requests is shown whereas in figure 6 depicts that neighboring feedback can significantly increase the streaming stability in a multistreaming end-to-end path.

Figures 7 shows the throughput evaluations under the Mean Total Transfer Delay (mean of all transfers for the total delay). The robustness of the throughput response under these measures is depicted when the Total Transfer Delay is increased, where the scheme is shown to be adequately behaving in the overall throughput offered, throughout the simulation.

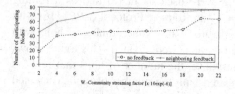
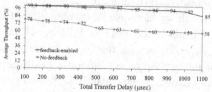

Fig. 6. Mean number of participating nodes in the intercluster feedback provision with the Community Streaming factor-W

Fig. 7. Throughput evaluation with the Mean Total Transfer Delay (mean of all transfers for the total delay)

5   Conclusions and Further Research

This work considers the modeled social interactions in the intercommunity domain enabling the created clusters to interact via social-oriented feedback as well as the existing individual movements of each node. The streaming is achieved through the collaborative outsourcing file chunk policy, where, in cooperation with the k-hop replication, the scheme avoids problems like file chunk redundancy and the increased utilization of storage resources. Experimental results show that the proposed scheme behaves satisfactory, allowing high SDR for completed files.

Current and future research directions include the modeling of the mobility pattern of the peers by using approaches like the fractional Brownian motion as well as other mobility schemes taking into account the global requests and different network partitioning parameters.

References

[1] Hui, P., Crowcroft, J., Yoneki, E.: BUBBLE Rap: Socialbased forwarding in Delay Tolerant Networks. In: Proceedings of the ACM MOBIHOC Conf., pp. 241–250 (2007)
[2] Zhang, M., Wolff, R.S.: Routing protocols for vehicular ad hoc networks in rural areas. IEEE Communications Magazine 46(11), 126–131 (2008)

[3] Hong, X., Xu, K., Gerla, M.: Scalable routing protocols for mobile ad hoc networks. IEEE Network Magazine 16(4), 11–21 (2002)

[4] Picconi, F., Massoulie, L.: Is There a Future for Mesh-Based live Video Streaming? In: Peer-to-Peer Computing 2008, pp. 289–298 (2008)

[5] Aguilera, M.K., Merchant, A., Shah, M., Veitch, A.C., Karamanolis, C.T.: Sinfonia: a new paradigm for building scalable distributed systems. In: 21st ACM Symposium on Operating Systems Principles (SOSP), SOSP 2007 ACM Symposium on Operating Systems Principles No 21, Stevenson, Washington, pp. 159–174. ETATS-UNIS (2007)

[6] Ko, Y.B., Vaidya, N.H.: Flooding-based geocasting protocols for mobile ad hoc networks. Mobile Networks and Applications 7(6), 471–480 (2002)

[7] Hara, T.: Effective replica allocation in ad hoc networks for improving data accessibility. In: Proceedings of IEEE INFOCOM, pp. 1568–1576. IEEE Computer Society (2001)

[8] Mavromoustakis, C., Karatza, H.: Reliable File Sharing Scheme for Mobile Peer-to-Peer Users Using Epidemic Selective Caching. In: Proceedings of IEEE International Conference on Pervasive Services (ICPS), Santorini, Greece, pp. 169–177 (July 2005)

[9] Mavromoustakis, C.X., Karatza, H.D.: Community oriented neighboring feedback for efficient end-to-end delay-sensitive MP2P streaming via temporal relay-based replication. Journal of Algorithms & Computational Technology 5(2), 177–198 (2011)

[10] Mavromoustakis, C.X., Karatza, H.D.: Dispersed information diffusion with level and schema-based coordination in mobile peer to peer networks. Cluster Computing (Computer Communications & Networks) 10(1), 33–45 (2007)

[11] Ko, Y.B., Vaidya, N.H.: Flooding-based geocasting protocols for mobile ad hoc networks. Mobile Networks and Applications 7(6), 471–480 (2002)

[12] Blough, D., Resta, G., Santi, P.: A Statistical Analysis of the Long-Run Node Spatial Distribution in Mobile Ad Hoc Networks. In: Wireless Networks vol. 10, pp. 543–554. Kluwer Academic Publishers (2004)

[13] Kulik, J., Heinzelman, W.R., Balakrishnan, H.: Negotiation-based protocols for disseminating information in wireless sensor networks. Wireless Networks 8(2-3), 169–185 (2002)

[14] Dembo, A., Peres, Y., Rosen, J., Zeitouni, O.: Thick points for spatial Brownian motion: multifractal analysis of occupation measure. Ann. Probab. 28(1), 1–35 (2000)

[15] Santi, P., Blough, D.: The critical transmitting range for connectivity in sparse wireless ad hoc networks. IEEE Transactions on Mobile Computing 2(1), 25–39 (2003)

[16] Haas, Z., Pearlman, M.: The performance of query control schemes for the zone routing protocol. ACM/IEEE Transactions on Networking 9(4), 427–438 (2001)

[17] Pemantle, R., Peres, Y.: What is the probability of intersecting the set of Brownian double points? Ann. Probab. 35, 2044–2062 (2007)

A Multi-touch Solution to Build Personalized Interfaces for the Control of Remote Applications

Gianluca Paravati[1], Mattia Donna Bianco[2], Andrea Sanna[1], and Fabrizio Lamberti[1]

[1] Politecnico di Torino, Dipartimento di Automatica e Informatica,
C.so Duca degli Abruzzi 24, I-10129, Torino, Italy
[2] CEDEO.net, Via Borgionera 103, I-10040, Villar Dora (TO), Italy
{gianluca.paravati,andrea.sanna,fabrizio.lamberti}@polito.it,
mattia@cedeo.net

Abstract. This paper presents a framework for controlling remote applications by means of personalized multi-touch interfaces. The designed framework allows end-users to fully personalize the mapping between gestures and input commands. A two-tier architecture has been developed. A formal description of the original interface is automatically generated at the server side to identify a set of available actions for controlling existing applications. The client is in charge of loading the description of the target application, allowing the user to shape the preferred mapping between gestures and actions. Finally, the server converts the identified actions into one or more commands understandable by the original computer interface. The implementation of the system for this work specifically relies on handheld multi-touch devices. Test results are encouraging, both from an objective and a subjective point of view; indeed, the designed framework resulted to outperform a traditional GUI both in terms of number of actions to perform a task and average completion time.

Keywords: Multi-Touch, personalized interfaces, human-machine interface, remote control.

1   Introduction

Human-machine interaction based on touch devices is quite common today. The evolution of input device technologies such as reflection-based or pressure-sensitive touch surfaces led to identification of the natural user interface (NUI) as the clear evolution of the human-machine interaction, following the shift from command-line interfaces (CLI) to graphical user interfaces (GUI).

The main goal of human-machine interaction is to improve the way users and computers communicate, by means of effective user interfaces. The design of user interfaces requires a careful mapping of complex user actions in order to make computers more intuitive, usable and receptive to the user's needs: in other words, more user-friendly.

Gestures, and in particular hand gestures, ever played a crucial role in human communication, as they constitute a direct expression of mental concepts [1]. The

F. Alvarez and C. Costa (Eds.): UCMEDIA 2010, LNICST 60, pp. 10–19, 2012.
© Institute for Computer Sciences, Social Informatics and Telecommunications Engineering 2012

naturalness and variety of hand gestures, compared with traditional interaction paradigms, can offer unique opportunities also for new and attracting forms of human-machine interaction [2]. Thus, new gesture-based paradigms are progressively introduced in various interaction scenarios (encompassing, for instance, navigation of virtual worlds, browsing of multimedia contents, management of immersive applications, etc. [3][4][21]), and the design of gesture-based systems will play an important role in the future trends of the human-computer interaction.

Indeed, we use gestures to express ourselves most of the times. Thus, GUI-based applications could be converted to take as input intuitive gestures. By means of a mapping between the original interface and the gesture-based one, applications could gain a higher degree of user friendliness, achieve better performance, and become easier to interact with. This new paradigm started to be introduced also for the control of consumer electronic devices. For instance, the CRISTAL project (Control of Remotely Interfaced Systems using Touch-based Actions in Living spaces) [5] enables people to control a wide variety of digital devices (TVs, music players, digital picture frames, speakers, light sources, etc.) from an interactive tabletop system that provides users with a gesture-based interface. User controls the devices through a virtually augmented representation of the surrounding environment.

Despite the evolution of the mobile world, most of the existing applications designed for the desktop world cannot run on mobile devices due to different hardware and graphics capabilities. One solution for allowing mobile user to access desktop-like applications involves the use of remote-computing techniques, where a remote server executes a specific application sending to the mobile device only the relevant graphics representation through a sequence of still images or a video stream [6][7]. This solution allows users to remotely control virtually any kind of application, including those that are still out of reach for handheld devices (as, for instance, the navigation in a 3D world composed by millions of polygons). Recently, a software independent approach extending the basic remote control paradigm to maintain a separate work area and user interface has been presented [8].

The aim of the proposed work is to describe a user-centric methodology to support the generalization of the mapping between existing GUIs and up-to-date NUIs, thus matching the above needs. To this purpose, the approach described in [8] is extended to build a solution supporting the creation of personalized and customizable human computer interaction interfaces by means of a generic gesture-based framework based on the multi-touch technology. The main advantage of the designed solution is that it allows for the development of user interfaces that most effectively and intuitively leverage one of the more relevant senses into the most optimal user friendliness (for instance, with projected-capacitive touch screen, users can give more complicated inputs like those used for sizing photos, adjusting web pages, etc.).

Basically, the framework is structured into a two-tier architecture. On one side, a server component is in charge of managing any kind of desktop application and to automatically build the description of its interface. This description is used to identify the functionalities of the target application and to create a personalized mapping between functionalities and user gestures that is then used for application control. Because of the availability of the 802.11g connectivity and of a mature set of APIs, in our test-bed the client side was implemented on the Apple's iPod Touch, one of the most popular multi-touch devices currently available on the market. However, the proposed approach is generic and can be applied to any kind of device able to capture user gestures.

This paper has been organized as follows. Section 2 reviews main works related to multi-touch interfaces. The proposed framework is described in Section 3. Section 4 presents a case study and the results of objective and subjective evaluations given by a set of users. Finally, conclusions and future works are discussed in Section 5.

2   Background

Recently, multi-touch technology has gained increasing attention both in the research community and the commercial world. On the market, various devices able to capture gestures already exist, ranging from tabletop displays to handheld devices. An in depth discussion on the application of multi-touch techniques for providing full control (6-DOFs) of a 3D rigid body using tabletop displays is reported in [9]. A different approach exploiting tabletop surfaces for designing a more realistic and sophisticated form of interaction is presented in [10].

The introduction of devices such as the Apple's iPhone and iPod Touch led researchers to focus their attention towards multi-touch user interfaces tailored to mobile environments. For instance, a framework to dispatch multi-touch events generated on a mobile device to a tabletop system is presented in [11]. Collaboration among users equipped with handheld multi-touch devices and tabletop frameworks is investigated in [12]. An interesting approach for manipulating 3D objects on multi-touch mobile devices has been recently presented in [13]. In this work, two iPod Touch units are attached back to back, and connected through a Wi-Fi connection; in this way, the freedom of manipulation is extended to a (pseudo) 3D scenario obtained by the sandwiched fixed volume architecture [14]. In [13] and [21], preliminary evaluations of the proposed interfaces are also carried out by collecting end-user feedbacks.

Gesture input on multi-touch handheld devices has not been used only for the control of desktop applications. As a matter of example, applications exploiting multi-touch technology to control IR devices are already available on the market. For instance, the RedEye system allows users to directly control devices such as TV, stereo, cable box, DVD player, and many other units that receive standard infrared signals by means of their iPhone or iPod Touch devices[15]. Similarly, in [16] iPhone and iPod Touch platforms are used for remote sensor control and data collection.

An interesting approach to adapt gesture input to the controlled application has been taken by the developers of SparshUI [17]. SparshUI is a platform-independent framework for developing multi-touch enabled applications, composed by a gesture server (in charge for handling the gesture processing), a gesture adapter (which is different for every controlled application), and an input device driver (that is needed to communicate with the gesture server). Drivers for several types of hardware devices have already been developed. Similarly, a software architecture supporting multi-touch capability on existing desktop systems, where both multi-touch and multiple single pointer inputs can be used simultaneously to manipulate existing application windows is proposed in [18]. The authors presented a proof-of-concept implementation of their architecture on the Linux system, demonstrating the possibility of using touch displays in a collaborative work environment.

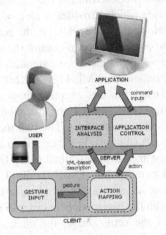

Fig. 1. Conceptual architecture of the designed multi-touch remote control system

The work presented in this paper follows a concept similar to SparshUI. However, it is aimed at enabling users to create their own multi-touch applications, whereas our intention is to adapt already existing applications to the multi-touch technology; for this reason, we need to create a description of the original interface and we lean on the results obtained in [8], where a software-independent framework, able to exploit image processing techniques to effectively decompose an original application into its main GUI elements, create a description of the original interface, and reload a personalized GUI on different devices, is presented.

3 The Proposed Framework

The proposed framework is structured into the two-tier architecture that is depicted in Figure 1. The user directly interacts with the client component, which is demanded to deal with all the aspects concerning gesture identification, interpretation, and personalization. On the other hand, the server interacts with the controlled application providing it with the translated gestures. The proposed solution requires a setup phase (indicated in Figure 1 by the dashed boxes), followed by the actual gesture mapping chain, composed by three steps, namely "Gesture Input", "Action Mapping" and "Application Control".

The setup phase is meant to create a formal description of the target application interface and it is composed by an off-line step (i.e. "Interface Analysis") and an on-line step (i.e. a part of the "Action Mapping" step). The off-line step is introduced for allowing the client application to know in advance which actions are associated to the target application. During the second step of the setup phase, the user will be able to personalize the mapping between gestures and available actions.

The interface of an existing application can be automatically analyzed through reverse engineering approaches in order to build a description of its elements. In this work, an image-based approach proposed in [9] has been used as the basis to design the "Interface Analysis" phase, which provides a method to create an XML-based description of the elements belonging to the GUI, i.e. the concrete aspects. Since other kinds of input methods can be possibly used to control the application, such as mouse or keyboard events, the method in [9] has been extended by introducing a language able to overcome the above issues. UsiXML [16], a XML-compliant User Interface Description Language, was used for this purpose: it is aimed at describing user interfaces according to four levels of abstraction: task model, abstract user interface, concrete user interface and final user interface. The two models describing tasks (i.e. actions) and the concrete aspects (buttons, keys, etc.) are of particular interest for the purpose of this work. The first model is described using UsiXML. The tasks can be composed by more sub-tasks; moreover, UsiXML allows to specify relationships among the tasks. The process of creating the complete description ends with the definition of a mapping between the two models in order to link them.

During the on-line step of the setup phase, the client device receives from the server a list of available applications and the corresponding XML-based descriptions. Once the target application has been selected, its XML-based description is loaded on the client device and the user can select a personalized gesture for each action. This step of the setup phase is aimed at creating a mapping between the multi-touch gestures (e.g. single, double, or multiple tap, pinch-in, pinch-out, joined or separate fingers, clockwise or counterclockwise rotations, etc.) and the described actions, which is stored into a conversion table. Moreover, during the setup phase the personalization of the multi-touch remote control is improved by allowing the user to select the preferred sensibility settings for each gesture.

The gesture mapping chain is split into two branches: "Gesture Input" and "Action Mapping" take place on the client device, whereas the "Application Control" logic is located on the server side. "Gesture Input" is oriented towards the human interface, taking as input the gestures drawn by the user on the multi-touch screen and delivering them to the next steps. During the intermediate step each recognized gesture is then translated into a meaningful action in the application context, based on the conversion table defined by the user during the setup phase, thus personalizing the new interface. On the other hand, the "Application Control" is part of the computer interface; each action received from the previous conversion block can be mapped into one or more input commands, which are then delivered to the target application. The original input can be either discrete (e.g., key presses) or continuous (e.g., mouse position, although digitized into a discrete quantity, is fast enough to be considered as continuous). To complete the description of the framework, a swim lane diagram showing, step-by-step, tasks involved in a client-server connection is presented in Figure 2.

At an early stage, a custom communication protocol has been defined for the management of all the events generated in the considered architecture, i.e. for the handling of the gesture association stage, the selection of the target application, the delivery of actions from the multi-touch device to the server, etc. However, it is worth observing that hardware devices and touch libraries are progressively adopting TUIO, an open standard recently introduced for structuring the description of touch event based communications [20] developed to provide hardware-independence. Therefore, it has been already planned the experimentation of the TUIO framework in the designed architecture.

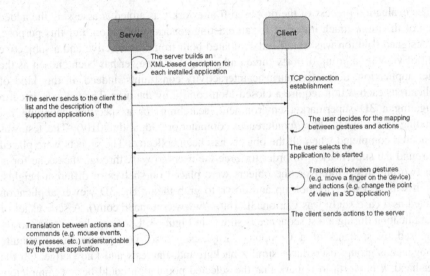

Fig. 2. Swim lane diagram of tasks involved in a client-server connection

4   A Case Study

The proposed framework has been implemented as a client-server application. The server application runs on a desktop PC with Microsoft Windows XP; with reference to Figure 1, the "Interface Analysis" and "Application Control" modules have been implemented in C++ language to be platform independent. The minimum requirements of the computer are determined by the target application to be controlled, since the server application has a very small footprint. The client application runs on an Apple iPodTouch device; it has been implemented in Objective-C language and Cocoa, the Apple's native object-oriented application development framework. The communication between the client and the server application occurs via a TCP connection and the handheld multi-touch device is connected to the desktop PC through a 802.11g wireless access point.

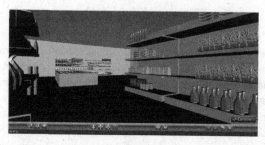

Fig. 3. Snapshot of the supermarket model used for testing the multi-touch interface

The evaluation process of the proposed framework was aimed at assessing the added value of the multi-touch interface for an existing generic application. For this purpose, the designed solution was tested and evaluated both from an objective and a subjective point of view by a group of forty-three end-users. A 3D viewer has been chosen as the target application, due to its intrinsic interactivity constraints; indeed, in this kind of applications each action require a closed-loop control by the user. The test consisted in navigating a 3D supermarket environment, searching for a specified shopping list including five objects (http://conferences.computer.org/3dui/3dui2010/). The test was considered completed when all the objects had been collected. The objects were placed all around the supermarket, in order to force the users to walk through the scene for at least two minutes. Moreover, the objects were placed on shelves of different heights; thus, it was necessary to look up and down to grab them. The 3D viewer application selected as a case study was Cortona3D (http://www.cortona3d.com/). A screenshot of the application during a test sequence is shown in Figure 3. User population was mostly composed by students of a Computer Graphics course, i.e. it represented a quite homogeneous group: users have similar background, interests and knowledge. On the other hand, it is worth to remark that the selected population could be not completely representative; in fact, students of the above course are already used to work with 3D computer graphics applications.

Only ten out of forty-three users owned a touch device. As their performances did not stand out, in the following they will not be discussed as a different group, but they will be kept together with the other.

Since the main interest during the case study was to evaluate the impact of the new user interface, the correlation due to the influence of the personalization of user gestures was minimized by choosing in advance default values both for sensibility and gesture mapping settings. Each user was individually trained on the execution of the test; then, each user was requested to complete the test both with the multi-touch device and the mouse. The tests were submitted with a random order, in order to limit the impact of the knowledge acquired during the first attempt on the overall result.

The overall usability and effectiveness of the experimented interface can be inferred from Table 1. The objective results were gathered focusing on the analysis of the average completion time and the average number of interactions needed to complete the task. In particular, each gesture was considered as a single interaction as well as each press-release of a button or key stroke, thus allowing to achieve a fair analysis of the two interfaces. The gesture-based framework resulted to outperform the traditional interface, both in terms of average completion time (13% improvement) and number of actions (18% saving).

The interest was not only on the objective data, but also on the subjective information (i.e., the impression that students had using the proposed interface). At the end of any test session, each user was asked to compile a brief questionnaire about the personal evaluation of the interfaces; in particular, the users were allowed to give a score ranging from one to four, with one indicating a forced/unnatural interface, and four meaning a very intuitive one. As shown in Table 1, the gesture-based solution appears to be significantly more user friendly than the original interface.

Table 1 also shows a statistical analysis on the experimental data that has been carried out to the purpose of disclosing the confidence level of the results obtained with the gesture based (GB) and the traditional (TR) interfaces. As variances are unknown and small samples are taken, the t-statistic was used to test the differences between the interfaces.

A paired t-test was performed by testing the hypothesis that the mean of differences between each pair of observation μ_t was $\mu_{GB}-\mu_{TR}=0$, both in terms of completion time, total number of interactions and subjective scores. As a rule of thumb, the risk level for computing the reference t-value for comparison was set to $\alpha=5\%$, finding a reference t-value equal to 1.99. According to the statistical analysis, as shown in Table 1, the t-statistic values computed for the comparison of the average number of actions and the subjective results were larger than the reference t-value; therefore, the null hypothesis could be rejected. Moreover, since the confidence level was larger than 99%, the proposed framework definitely showed to outperform the traditional interface. On the other hand, the t-statistic value computed for the time comparison resulted to be lower than the reference t-value. As a matter of fact, in the latter case the null hypothesis (with $\alpha=5\%$) could not be rejected. Although the decrease in user actions and the increase in the degree of user satisfaction could be specifically related to the adoption of the gesture-based framework, the saving in time might be not fully related to the same fact (a confidence level equal to 70% was reached). This could be explained by considering the relation between the type of tasks that users needed to perform and the size of the input device: as already outlined in [21], actions that need a high level of precision can not be accurately controlled by multi-touch mobile device.

Table 1. Objective and subjective results indicating the performance using the traditional interface and the gesture-based framework. All the results are expressed as average values.

Interface	Objective Results		Subjective Results
	Time	Actions	User evaluation
Traditional	252 s	138	2.65
Gesture-based	218 s	113	3.23
Statistics:			
Gesture-based improvement	13%	18%	18%
t-statistic value	1.05	3.69	3.59
confidence level	70%	99%	99%

5   Conclusions and Future Works

A customizable and portable human computer interaction interface has been presented in this paper. The framework exploits a gesture-based paradigm relying on the multi-touch technology and it is aimed at controlling existing applications by translating the original command inputs into gestures that can be customized by the user. The main reason behind the measured improvement is that by using gestures an immediate and more intuitive access to the action to be performed can be achieved.

Future works will be aimed at investigating the use of gesture-based interfaces to control real-time applications (e.g. to supervise a robot). Moreover, further experiments involving larger multi-touch input devices are planned, with the aim of checking if it is possible to reduce the limitations identified during the execution of high precision tasks.

Acknowledgment. This article is part of a work developed within the frame of the project "Piattaforma Tecnologica Innovativa per l'Internet of Things" co-funded by the Regione Piemonte.

References

1. Pavlovi'c, V.I., Sharma, R., Huang, T.S.: Visual interpretation of hand gestures for human-computer interaction: a review. IEEE TPAMI 19, 677–695 (1997)
2. Pavlovi'c, V.I., Sharma, R., Huang, T.S.: Gestural interface to a visual computing environment for molecular biologists. In: Proc. of the 2nd Intern. Conf. on Automatic Face and Gesture Recognition, pp. 52–73. IEEE Computer Society, Los Alamitos (1996)
3. Selker, T.: Touching the future. Commun. ACM 51, 14–16 (2008)
4. Wright, A.: Making sense of sensors. Commun. ACM 52, 14–15 (2009)
5. Seifried, T., Rendl, C., Perteneder, F., Leitner, J., Haller, M., Sakamoto, D., Kato, J., Inami, M., Scott, S.D.: CRISTAL, control of remotely interfaced systems using touch-based actions in living spaces. In: SIGGRAPH 2009 Emerging Technologies, N.Y. (2009)
6. Gong, J., Tarasewich, P.: Guidelines for Handheld Mobile Device Interface Design. In: Proc. Decision Sciences Inst., Decision Sciences Inst., pp. 3751–3756 (2004)
7. Florins, M., Vanderdonckt, J.: Graceful Degradation of User Interfaces as a Design Method for Multiplatform Systems. In: Proc. 9th ACM Int'l Conf. IUI 2004, pp. 140–147 (2004)
8. Lamberti, F., Sanna, A.: Extensible GUIs for Remote Application Control on Mobile Devices. IEEE Computer Graphics and Applications 28(4), 50–57 (2008)
9. Hancock, M., Carpendale, S., Cockburn, A.: Shallow-depth 3D interaction: design and evaluation of one, two and threetouch techniques. In: CHI 2007: Proceedings of the SIGCHI Conference on Human Factors in Computing Systems, pp. 1147–1156. ACM, N.Y (2007)
10. Wilson, A.D., Izadi, S., Hilliges, O., Garcia-Mendoza, A., Kirk, D.: Bringing physics to the surface. In: UIST 2008: Proceedings of the 21st Annual ACM Symposium on User Interface Software and Technology, pp. 67–76. ACM, New York (2008)
11. Hafeneger, S., Weiss, M., Herkenrath, G., Borchers, J.: Pockettable: Mobile devices as multi-touch controllers for tabletop application development. Extended Abstracts of Tabletop 2008 (2008)

12. Nestler, S., Echtler, F., Dollinger, A., Klinker, G.: Collaborative problem solving on mobile hand-held devices and stationary multi-touch interfaces. In: PPD 2008: Workshop on Designing Multitouch Interaction Techniques for Coupled Public and Private Displays (2008)
13. Shen, E.L., Tsai, S.S., Chu, H.H., Hsu, J., Chen, C.W.: Double-side multi-touch input for mobile devices. In: CHI 2009: Proceedings of the SIGCHI. ACM, New York (2009)
14. Wigdor, D., Leigh, D., Forlines, C., Shipman, S., Barnwell, J., Balakrishnan, R., Shen, C.: Under the table interaction. In: UIST 2006: Proc. of the 19th Annual ACM Symposium on User Interface Software and Technology, pp. 259–268. ACM, New York (2006)
15. RedEye, http://thinkflood.com/products/redeye/what-is-redeye/
16. Geltz, B.R., Berlier, J.A., McCollum, J.M.: Using the iPhone and iPod Touch for remote sensor control and data acquisition. In: IEEE Proc. of the SoutheastCon, pp. 9–12 (2010)
17. Sparsh-UI, http://code.google.com/p/sparsh-ui/
18. Cheng, K., Itzstein, B., Sztajer, P., Rittenbruch, P.: A unified multi-touch & multi-pointer software architecture for supporting collocated work on the desktop. Technical Report ATP-2247. NICTA, Australian Technology Park, Sydney, Australia (2009)
19. Limbourg, Q., Vanderdonckt, J., Michotte, B., Bouillon, L., López-Jaquero, V.: USIXML: A Language Supporting Multi-path Development of User Interfaces. In: Feige, U., Roth, J. (eds.) DSV-IS 2004 and EHCI 2004. LNCS, vol. 3425, pp. 200–220. Springer, Heidelberg (2005)
20. Kaltenbrunner, M., Bovermann, T., Bencina, R., Costanza, E.: TUIO: A Protocol for Table-Top Tangible User Interfaces. In: 6th International Gesture Workshop (2005)
21. Fiorella, D., Sanna, A., Lamberti, F.: Multi-touch user interface evaluation for 3D object manipulation on mobile devices. Journal on Multimodal User Interfaces (2009)

Semantic Characterization of Context of Use and Contents for User-Centric Media Retrieval

Juan Carlos Yelmo García, Yod Samuel Martín García,
and Beatriz San Miguel González

Universidad Politécnica de Madrid, Ciudad Universitaria s/n, 28040 Madrid, Spain
{jcyelmo,samuelm,smiguel}@dit.upm.es

Abstract. When users access online media, they need and desire to get an experience tailored to their specific, personal context and situation. This is becoming more and more relevant with the ever-increasing amount of available contents users may choose from. In order to provide user-centric functionalities (such as relevant searches, content adaptation, customization and recommendation), both the annotation of contents with semantically rich metadata and an accurate model of the individual users and their respective contexts of use are needed. In this context, we propose a solution to automatically characterize both the context of use and the contents. It provides dynamic, adaptive user models, with explicit and implicit information; as well as content descriptors that may be later used to match the most suitable contents for each user. Users always keep a pivotal role throughout the whole process: providing new contents, contributing to moderated folksonomies, overseeing their own user model, etc.

Keywords: annotation, metadata, user model, content description, adaptation, customization, personalized search.

1   Introduction: The Need for Semantic Characterization

Users are already accustomed to access contents anywhere, anytime and from any device. Nowadays, they expect to get an experience personalized to their specific preferences and needs –which may also vary with their context or the tasks they are performing at each moment. The answer to this demand lies in user-centric tools, which adapt their functionalities to each user, and keep them in permanent control of the process, whereas reducing the cognitive load to a minimum.

The contents of this paper belong to a broader project where a multimedia search engine is being developed [1]. We are presenting a work in progress that is aimed at offering a framework to enhance existing search functionalities with user-centric features, as well as to provide new operations, namely:

- *User-centric search*: defined as the selection of a reduced subset of contents from a large repository, based on some structured or unstructured indications provided by the user (in the form of a search query). Implicit inputs from the user model may improve search accuracy, relevance and correction.

F. Alvarez and C. Costa (Eds.): UCMEDIA 2010, LNICST 60, pp. 20–25, 2012.

- *Recommendation*: same as *search*, but without any active intervention from the user (recommendation is push-mode, initiated by the platform without any other inputs).
- *Customization*: selection of one type of media from a reduced set of equivalent contents (e.g., versions of the same content)
- *Adaptation*: transformation of a concrete input content (this is the only operation where the content itself is delivered to the user, rather than mere pointers to it).

The foundations of the user-centric features are the same for each operation. The search engine relies on rich, semantic descriptions of both the user accessing it and the contents from a (distributed or centralized) repository. Given those descriptions, a *match* operation is performed that selects the best available contents for the particular user. Consequently, a structured knowledge needs to be obtainable about both the users (to know their needs and preferences) and the contents (to assess how they fit for a specific user) [2]. Specifically, we propose a semantic framework that captures, represents and stores those two kinds of knowledge, so that the engine may use it to provide user-centric functionalities. This framework is ancillary to the search engine, providing a repository of user and content metadata that may be applied to user-centric functionalities. Figure 1 summarizes all the elements of our framework, how they interrelate and connect to each other and the role the user plays with respect to each component.

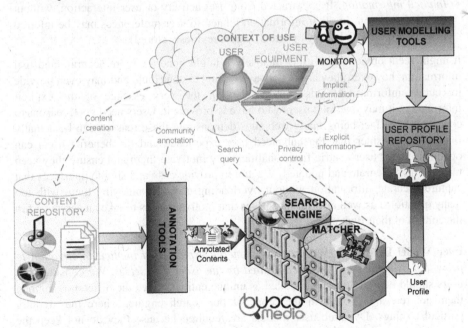

Fig. 1. A Search Engine is augmented with a Matcher module that provides user-centric features. The Matcher relies on information about both contents (provided by the annotation tools) and users (retrieved from the User Profile Repository). Users may play an active role in all the stages of this process.

2   Modelling the User and the Context of Use

In order to provide the aforementioned user-centric functionalities, the search engine requires a model of each of the individual users accessing it [3]. This model is a computational description of a certain user in a system that includes relevant information of the user, providing a structured knowledge of their activities, preferences and capacities. To get a real picture, our user models not only deal with users themselves, but they also cover the rest of the elements appearing in their context of use: knowledge, expertise, goals, culture, preferences, behaviour, dexterous and sensory capabilities, organization, ambience, software and hardware platform, etc.

Next, we describe how this information is collected and we introduce the user model we are considering in our engine, together with the research challenges it might entail.

Capturing User Information. We may distinguish two types of user information regarding the way it is gathered:

- *Explicit information*: Users personally input it through forms or opinion polls. It may include demographic information, ratings, written opinions, etc.
- *Implicit information*: It is extracted from user activity or user interaction, without their intervention. Implicit information related to user preferences may be inferred from user browsing history or search logs (previously stored).

It might seem obvious that users themselves might generate more accurate and real information; however, they are not always willing to contribute and may even provide inaccurate information. This problem lies in the very essence of the explicit information: it may overload users who have to provide it. Users need good reasons to contribute –the fact being many web sites demonstrate these reasons can be actually found. We consider that the enhanced user experience and the benefits users can obtain from our user-centric functionalities may motivate them and ensure they keep their profiles accurate and updated. We aim to provide easy and simple interfaces that capture accurate information without overloading users or annoying them with too many questions; as well as offer incentives that motivate users to take an active part in the control of their own model.

User Model Definition. We propose to *merge explicit and implicit information to provide a dynamic user model controlled by the users themselves*. We consider that users should be individually modelled as unique entities, since the differences among them are relevant enough in the scope of our search engine, where they require particular things. Dynamic user models are required because they do not keep the same information over time and they can be modified, amplified or improved to adapt to circumstances –and therefore, to the different users. In short, the major advantage of these models is just this last point: they allow characterizing users individually, since they adapt better to different users [4]. We may anticipate that several approaches we will employ will be based on the probabilistic inference of the user features (e.g. Bayesian networks, clustering around user stereotypes, collaborative filtering, etc).

Furthermore, as we mentioned before, we aim at providing users with control of their own user model. In this sense, based on the work of [5], we propose to incorporate appropriate interfaces that clearly present user information stored through an open user model. This open model also incorporates tools that allow users to oversee, modify and delete their information. It is important to point out that the user information that users can control is not only explicit information stored, but also information inferred by the engine. Furthermore, by changing this information, users may feed explicit information back to their user model, whose accuracy and validity will thus increase. If conflicts between explicit and implicit information appear, they will be solved probabilistically, nonetheless, the users will keep the last word on which information the model stores about them.

Users may benefit as well from this open model, since they can control and safeguard their privacy by watching, modifying and deleting their personal data in a transparent and clear way, which we think could be a reason to increase their participation in the collection of user information.

3   Annotating the Contents

Three issues must be tackled regarding content annotations: their scope, their generation and their representation.

Scope: what should the metadata denote? In the scope of our project, we aim to get descriptors that: (a) are relevant to the operations mentioned in section 1, and (b) can entail constraints upon the context of use. For instance, we are considering these kinds of descriptors:

- *Semantic labels*: topics addressed by the content, domain of the context, named entities appearing in the content, etc.
- *Context*: date and location depicted in the content.
- *Presentation characteristics*: rendering modalities, media format, and natural language.

Generation: how do we get metadata? In order to generate the content description, a direct option would be to analyze the contents every time they are being accessed; however, this turns out impractical because of its associated computational load. Instead, we propose a threefold approach to generate metadata used to annotate contents:

1. *Manual or assisted annotation by content producers.* Ideally, contents would be provided with semantic annotations attached during production (be by either the author or another member of the producer's team). However, this is not always feasible, especially when contents are created by non-professional prosumers [6].

2. *Content augmentation by the community.* Metadata may be adjoined to contents after they have been created. This may leverage on crowd wisdom to have annotations provided by users, each of whom may add a small bit of metadata. Examples of this practice are the folksonomies [7] (that label contents with semantic tags) and social accessibility [8] (where contents are enriched with hints for assistive technologies). We expect to have community annotations rely on automatic moderation tools to funnel the community, so as to ensure the quality and relevance of the annotations they generate and constrain them to partially controlled vocabularies that ease further processing.

3. *Automated generation and storage of annotations by analytic tools.* The cheapest way to add annotations is the automation of this process. The process may rely on external tools that perform activities ranging from the mere extraction of embedded metadata to linguistic analysis, object recognition, heuristic accessibility evaluation, etc.

Representation: how is metadata stored and transmitted? The metadata that annotates contents should be represented in a standard way that allows it to be reused by any tool, disregarding what original content it refers to. We have considered several, complementary alternatives:

- Generic, vocabulary-independent models such as the Protocol for Web Description Resources [9] (POWDER), which allows for easily integrating information on different domains (accessibility, adult-oriented content restrictions, mobile access, etc.)
- Multimedia content description standards such as MPEG-7.
- Bibliographic information models such as Dublin Core, Machine Reading Cataloging (MARC), Medatata Object Description Schema (MODS), or the Text Encoding Initiative.
- Multimedia news-oriented metadata formats, such as the Information Interchange Module and NewsML.

We must remark that all these different formats are easy to integrate in a generic framework by leveraging on generic models (such as the aforesaid POWDER), since all of them are controlled vocabularies which also define a representation as XML.

4   Conclusions and Future Work

We have explained how user-centric content search, selection and recovery tools may take advantage of a proper characterization of contents and users to improve their results. A work in progress has been presented to explain a framework that collects, stores and represents metadata that may be used by those tools. This framework may be qualified as user-centric, because not only it eases a personalized access to contents, but it also puts the users in control of the whole annotation process, letting them decide how involved they would be:

- Content annotation may range from being specified during production time, to being fully automated, to even rely on other users socially augmenting it.
- User models may be built up exclusively from inferred information, but they also rely on user-provided information. Moreover, privacy-concerned users may always limit and specify the information stored about them at each moment.

As the work herein presented continues, the annotation framework implementation will be completed, possibly integrating external tools to analyze contents and user logs, and finally they will be integrated into the search, selection and recovery tools.

Acknowledgments. The works herein presented are being developed as part of the Buscamedia project of the CENIT-E programme, with reference number CEN-20091026, partially funded by the CDTI (Centro para el Desarrollo Tecnológico e Industrial), supported by the Spanish Ministry of Science and Innovation. The authors would like to thank the knowledge and the contributions of the Buscamedia consortium partners (www.cenitbuscamedia.es). This part of the project has been specifically contracted to Universidad Politécnica de Madrid by GFI Informática.

References

1. Cenit Buscamedia. Project Page, http://www.cenitbuscamedia.es/
2. Moura, J., Chainho, P., Damásio, C.V.: Semantically Enabled Framework for User Centric Profile Description, Search and Match. In: Di Nitto, E., Ripeanu, M. (eds.) ICSOC 2007. LNCS, vol. 4907, pp. 326–335. Springer, Heidelberg (2009)
3. Rich, E.: Users are individuals: individualizing user models. Int. J. Hum.-Comput. Stud. 51(2), 323–338 (1999)
4. Gaudioso, E., Boticario, J.G.: User Data Management and Usage Model Acquisition in an Adaptive Educational Collaborative Environment. In: De Bra, P., Brusilovsky, P., Conejo, R. (eds.) AH 2002. LNCS, vol. 2347, pp. 143–152. Springer, Heidelberg (2002)
5. Ahn, J., Brusilovsky, P., Grady, J., He, D., Syn, S.Y.: Open user profiles for adaptive news systems: help or harm? In: Proceedings of the 16th International Conference on World Wide Web Banff, Alberta, Canada, May 08-12, pp. 11–20. ACM, New York (2007)
6. Participative Web and User-Created Content: Web 2.0, Wikis and Social Networking. SourceOCDE Science et technologies de l'information, 2007, 15. OECD Organisation for Economic Co-operation and Development (2007)
7. Halpin, H., Robu, V., Shepherd, H.: The complex dynamics of collaborative tagging. In: Proceedings of the 16th International Conference on World Wide Web, WWW 2007 Banff, Alberta, Canada, May 08-12, pp. 211–220. ACM, New York (2007)
8. Sato, D., Kobayashi, M., Takagi, H., Asakawa, C.: Social accessibility: the challenge of improving web accessibility through collaboration. In: Proceedings of the 2010 International Cross Disciplinary Conference on Web Accessibility (W4a), W4A 2010 Raleigh, North Carolina, April 26-27, ACM, New York (2010)
9. Archer, P., Smith, K., Perego, A. (eds.): Protocol for Web Description Resources (POWDER): Description Resources, W3C Recommendation. W3C (2009), http://www.w3.org/TR/powder-dr/

Towards the Creation of a Unified Framework for Multimodal Search and Retrieval

Apostolos Axenopoulos, Petros Daras, and Dimitrios Tzovaras

Centre for Research and Technology Hellas, Informatics and Telematics Institute,
6th Km Charilaou-Thermi Road Rd., 57001, Thermi, Thessaloniki, Greece
{axenop,daras,tzovaras}@iti.gr

Abstract. In this paper, a novel framework for search and retrieval of multimodal content is introduced as part of the EU-funded project I-SEARCH. The main objective of I-SEARCH is to create a unified framework for multimodal content search, i.e. to retrieve content of any media type (text, 2D images, video, audio and 3D) by using as query any of the above media, along with real-world information, expressive and social cues. The outcome will be a highly user-centric search engine, able to deliver to the end-users only the content of interest, satisfying their information needs and preferences, which is expected to significantly improve end-user's experience. The paper will present the concept of I-SEARCH, as well as its major scientific advances.

Keywords: Multimodal Content Search and Retrieval, user-centric search engine, RUCoD.

1   Introduction

Multimedia content, which is available over the Internet, is increasing at a rate faster than the respective increase of computational power and storage capabilities. Due to the widespread availability of digital recording devices, improved modeling tools, advanced scanning mechanisms as well as display and rendering devices, even over mobile environments, users are more and more empowered to live a more immersive and unforgettable experience with last-generation digital media, through experiencing audiovisual content. It is therefore now possible for users to rapidly move from a mainly textual-based to a media-based "embodied" Internet, where rich audiovisual content (images, sound, videos), 3D representations (avatars) and reconstructions, virtual and mixed reality worlds, serious games, life-logging applications, multimodal yet affective utterances (gestures, facial expressions, eye movements, etc.) become a reality.

This growth of popularity of media is not accompanied by the rapid development of media search technologies. The most popular media services in the Web are typically limited to textual search [1, 2]. However, the last years, significant efforts have been devoted, mainly by the European research community, for achieving

F. Alvarez and C. Costa (Eds.): UCMEDIA 2010, LNICST 60, pp. 26–34, 2012.

content-based search of images [6, 8, 9, 10], video [7, 11, 12, 13, 14] and 3D models [3, 15, 16, 17, 18]. Same endeavors are also lately noticed by the big players in these fields (Google image, Google SketchUp [4]).

Despite the significant achievements in multimedia search technologies, the existing solutions still lack several important features, which could guarantee high-quality search services and improved end-user experience. These features are listed below:

- A unified framework for multimodal content search and retrieval: this will enable users express their queries in any form most suitable for them, retrieve content in various forms providing the user with a complete view of the retrieved information and interact with the content using the most suitable modality for the particular user and under the specific context each time.
- Sophisticated mechanisms for interaction with content: these will exploit at best the social and collaborative behavior of users interacting with the content, which will enable them to better express what they want to retrieve.
- Efficient presentation of the retrieved results: this will optimally present to the user the most relevant results according to the query and the user preferences.

Towards this direction, the I-SEARCH project [5] aims to provide a novel unified framework for multimedia and multimodal content indexing, search and retrieval. The I-SEARCH framework will be able to handle specific types of multimedia (text, 2D image, sketch, video, 3D objects, audio and combination of the above) and support multimodal interaction means (gestures, face expressions, eye movements) along with real world information (GPS, temperature, time, weather sensors, RFID objects,), which can be used as queries and retrieve any available relevant content of any of the aforementioned types and from any end-user access device. Furthermore I-SEARCH will be able to integrate even non-verbal yet implicit, emotional cues, and social descriptors, in order to better express what the user wants to retrieve.

The proposed search engine is expected to be highly user-centric in the sense that only the content of interest will be delivered to the end-users, satisfying their information needs and preferences, which is expected to dramatically improve end-user experience. Furthermore, I-SEARCH introduces the use of advanced visual analytic technologies for search results presentation in order to facilitate their fast and easy interpretation and also to support optimal results presentation under various contexts (i.e. user profile, end-user terminal, available network bandwidth, interaction modality preference, etc.).

In the following, a description of the I-SEARCH concept and the project's main objectives is initially provided, followed by the major scientific advances proposed by I-SEARCH, such as the Rich Unified Content Description (RUCoD), Multimodal Annotation Propagation, Multimodal Interaction and Visualization.

2   I-SEARCH Objectives and Conceptual Architecture

The aim of the I-SEARCH project is the development of the first search engine able to handle a wide range of specific types of multimedia and multimodal content (text, 2D image, sketch, video, 3D objects, audio and combination of the above), which can be used as queries and retrieve any available relevant content of any of the aforementioned types.

2.1   I-SEARCH Objectives

Towards the realization of the first multimodal search engine, I-SEARCH introduces the concept of Rich Unified Content Description (RUCoD). RUCoD will consist of a multi-layered structure (from low-level to high-level descriptors), which will integrate content's geometrical, topological, temporal, multisensory and multimodal information and meta-tags connected with the intrinsic properties of the content (static features such as shape, colour, texture, dimension, etc.), dynamic properties (temporal descriptors, how it behaves, in which activities it is normally used, who uses it, etc.), non-verbal expressive and emotional descriptors, social descriptors (how content is related to users, social/collaborative use of the content), content descriptors as for the behavior of the humans included in the (visual and vocal) content, descriptors for users' behavior as for how content is intended to be elaborated and manipulated, individually or socially. Further, novel multimodal annotation propagation algorithms will be developed, i.e. annotating information of one form/modality using information describing other forms/modalities of the same object.

Furthermore, the development of intelligent content interaction mechanisms is proposed, so that only the content of interest will be delivered to the users. This will be achieved by providing users with natural and expressive and multimodal interfaces as well as through personal and social-based relevance (including recommendation-based) feedback mechanisms. In this context, social and collaborative behavior of users interacting with the content will be exploited at best, which will help users to better express what they want to retrieve.

Finally, I-SEARCH will provide a novel way for presentation of the multimodal data retrieved by the search engine, by utilizing visual analytics technologies. The unified content representation will be exploited for generating advanced reasoning algorithms to drive the visualization of the I-SEARCH RUCoD-compliant content. Visual Analytics will provide an analytical process for presenting the search results in the optimal way to aid the user in finding the result that optimally matches the query in a fast and efficient way.

2.2   I-SEARCH Architecture

The overall conceptual architecture of I-SEARCH is shown in the figure below:

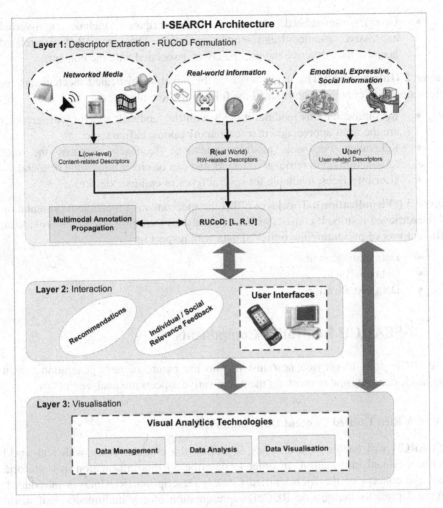

Fig. 1. The I-SEARCH Architecture

The three distinct layers of the I-SEARCH conceptual architecture are analyzed in the sequel.

Layer 1 (Descriptor Extraction – RUCoD Formulation): This layer includes all the descriptor extraction mechanisms, which lead to the novel RUCoD descriptor. Three main types of descriptors constitute the unified RUCoD descriptor:

- L(ow-level), content-related descriptors: L-descriptors are directly extracted from the networked media (text, audio, image, video and 3D), by utilizing low-level feature extraction mechanisms.
- R(eal world) - related descriptors: R-descriptors refer to the real world information captured from various sensors integrated in the environment. Such sensors include GPS, temperature, time, weather sensors, RFID objects, etc.

- U(ser), user-related descriptors: U-descriptors include non-verbal expressive, emotional and social descriptors. They are called user-related because they describe the user behavior associated with the content.

Layer 2 (Interaction): This layer involves the novel sophisticated mechanisms for interaction with content. It consists of the following three modules:

- Recommendations module: it deals with the feedback added by experts that are the most appreciated in a community upon a define topic.
- Relevance Feedback module: relevance feedback captures the user satisfaction upon retrieval of results and can be either individual or social.
- User interfaces, available for several types of end-user devices.

Layer 3 ((Visualization): This layer offers the mechanisms for efficient presentation of the retrieved results. It consists of Visual Analytics technologies, which provide an efficient way of presenting the retrieved data with respect to:

- Data management.
- Data analysis.
- Data visualization.

3   I-SEARCH Innovative Components

I-SEARCH aims to provide new insight into the nature of next generation search engines for audiovisual content. Its main innovative aspects are analyzed below.

3.1   A Rich Unified Content Description (RUCoD)

I-SEARCH will handle several types of multimedia content, along with real-world and user-related information. In order to describe all this information in a uniform way, the concept of the Rich Unified Content Description (RUCoD) is introduced. Figure 2 presents the generic RUCoD representation of any multimedia, real world and user-related information supported by the I-SEARCH system.

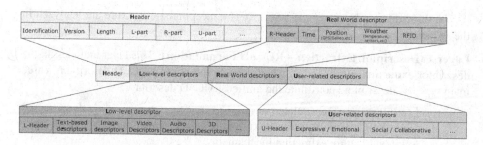

Fig. 2. The RUCoD Format

The major advantage of RUCoD is that it enables to easily link information from different media, e.g., a music piece can be linked with video, text documents, and possible further related material, a 3D object can be linked with text, 2D images, video and so on. In this way, search and retrieval of multimedia content is treated in a unified manner, i.e. users will be able to use as query any of the RUCoD-supported media types (text, 2D image, sketch, video, 3D objects and audio) and retrieve any available relevant content of any of the aforementioned types.

Beyond the intrinsic properties of the multimedia documents, RUCoD will also support descriptors related to expressive/emotional and social cues, multisensory and real world information. Whereas traditional content-based retrieval systems only extract and take into account either low-level features of the media data or descriptors of user's preferences, the search engine featured in I-SEARCH will also consider the multisensory information (user's gesture, mood, time, location, etc.) associated with the content.

3.2 Multimodal Annotation Propagation

Multimodal annotation propagation deals with annotating information of one form using information describing other forms of the object. More specifically, the automatic multimodal annotation propagation will be applied to non-available content and to non-available description of the RUCoD, which means that if some of the types of content describing an object are not available, or the user hasn't added metadata, the system will learn from past history/use of the object itself or similarity with other objects and will propagate this data to the empty cells of the RUCoD. Figure 3 shows an example of multimodal annotation propagation (the user adds metadata to an image described in RUCoD and the system propagates this information to annotate also all other types of information contained in the database that are linked to the specific image).

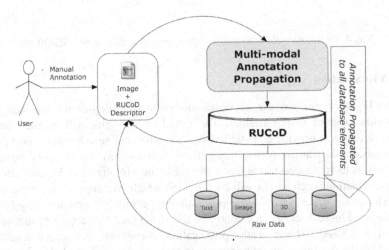

Fig. 3. Multimodal annotation propagation example

3.3   Multimodal Interaction

Multimodal interaction refers to novel, sophisticated mechanisms and interfaces for embodied interaction with content, with a main focus on multimodality (including non-verbal, full-body), context-awareness, and emotional/expressive interaction. Natural and expressive interfaces will be based on analysis of user's movement and gesture.

A preliminary block diagram of the interaction module of I-SEARCH is shown in Figure 4. The interoperability of the module with the remaining I-SEARCH components is assured through the representation of the high-, mid- and low-level interaction descriptors in RUCoD. The interaction manager module caters for interfacing the I-SEARCH interaction module with the networked media descriptor extraction and the visualisation modules of I-SEARCH.

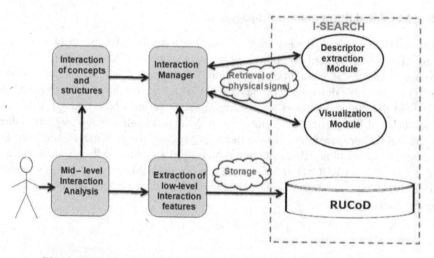

Fig. 4. Preliminary block diagram of the interaction module of I-SEARCH

3.4   Visualization

I-SEARCH introduces the use of visual analytics technologies for enhancing the presentation layer of search engines. The visual technologies will be built upon a framework that will provide analytic reasoning methods of search results. Novel data representation and transformation mechanisms will convert the RUCoD format of search results to structured forms that will enable the visualization. Finally, adaptive visual presentation mechanisms will be provided which will support the presentation of search results under various contexts utilizing various information visualization technologies. Figure 5 shows an example of the visual analytics approach that will be followed in I-SEARCH for results presentation. As shown, the search results are analyzed by the reasoning module in order to extract relevant knowledge that is then used for the transformation of the results to the appropriate format and the subsequent presentation of the results using the most appropriate visualization method.

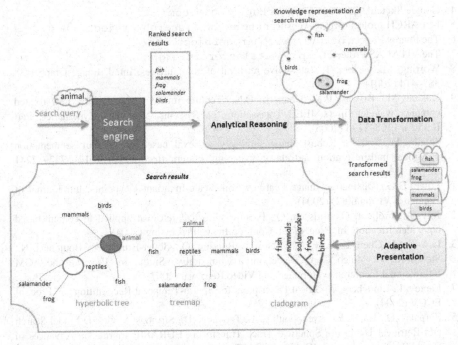

Fig. 5. The Visual Analytics Approach

4   Conclusions

In this paper, a novel framework to multimedia search engines has been introduced. Through the realization of the I-SEARCH project, numerous cutting-edge technologies are going to revolutionize the way multimedia search over the Internet is performed. After an overview of the conceptual architecture of I-SEARCH, an analysis of its main innovative components followed. These include specification of a Rich Unified Content Description (RUCoD), Multimodal Annotation Propagation, Multimodal Interaction mechanisms and novel results presentation capabilities. The I-SEARCH framework will be able to handle at the same time several types of multimedia (text, 2D image, sketch, video, 3D objects, audio and combination of the above) and multimodal content (gestures, face expressions, eye movements) along with real world information (GPS, temperature, time, weather sensors, RFID objects, etc.). Finally, the search engine will be dynamically adapted to end-user's device, which will vary from a simple mobile phone to a high-performance PC.

References

1. Flickr Photo Sharing, http://www.flickr.com/
2. Internet Archive, http://www.archive.org/
3. VICTORY project official website,
   http://www.victory-eu.org:8080/victory

4. Google SketchUp, http://sketchup.google.com/
5. I-SEARCH project official website, http://www.isearch-project.eu/
6. The Pharos Project, http://www.pharosproject.net/
7. The VITALAS Project, http://vitalas.ercim.org/
8. Worring, M., Gevers, T.: Interactive retrieval of color images. Int. J. Image Graph 1(3), 387–414 (2001)
9. Kokare, M., Biswas, P.K., Chatterji, B.N.: Texture image retrieval using new rotated complex wavelet filters. IEEE Transactions on Systems, Man, and Cybernetics, Part B 35(6), 1168–1178 (2005)
10. Attalla, E., Siy, P.: Robust shape similarity retrieval based on contour segmentation polygonal multiresolution and elastic matching. Pattern Recognition 38(12), 2229–2241 (2005)
11. Lowe, D.G.: Distinctive Image Features from Scale-Invariant Keypoints. Int. Journal of Computer Vision 60(2) (2004)
12. Joly, A., Frélicot, C., Buisson, O.: Feature statistical retrieval applied to content-based copy identification. In: Proc. of Int. Conf. on Image Processing (2004)
13. Law-To, J., Chen, L., Joly, A., Laptev, I., Buisson, O., Gouet-Brunet, V., Boujemaa, N., Stentiford, F.: Video Copy Detection: a Comparative Study. In: Proc. of the ACM International Conference on Image and Video Retrieval (2007)
14. Laptev, I., Lindeberg, T.: Local Descriptors for Spatio-Temporal Recognition. In: Proc. of ECCV (2004)
15. Zarpalas, D., Daras, P., Axenopoulos, A., Tzovaras, D., Strintzis, M.G.: 3D Model Search and Retrieval Using the Spherical Trace Transform., EURASIP Journal on Advances in Signal Processing, Article ID 239110 (2007)
16. Papadakis, P., Pratikakis, I., Perantonis, S., Theoharis, T.: Efficient 3D shape matching and retrieval using a concrete radialized spherical projection representation. Pattern Recognition 40(9), 2437–2452 (2007)
17. Daras, P., Axenopoulos, A.: A 3D Shape Retrieval Framework Supporting Multimodal Queries. International Journal of Computer Vision (July 2009), doi:10.1007/s11263-009-0277-2
18. Ohbuchi, R., Osada, K., Furuya, T., Banno, T.: Salient local visual features for shape-based 3D model retrieval. In: Proc. of the IEEE International Conference on Shape Modeling and Applications (SMI 2008), pp. 93–102 (2008)

Multimodal Queries to Access Multimedia Information Sources: First Steps[*]

Ángel Martínez[1], Sara Lana Serrano[1], José L. Martínez-Fernández[1,2], and Paloma Martínez[2]

[1] DAEDALUS, Data, Decisions And Language, S.A.
Avda. de la Albufera, 321, 28031 Madrid, Spain
{amartinez,slana,jmartinez}@daedalus.es
[2] Advanced Databases Group, Universidad Carlos III de Madrid
Avda. de la Universidad, 30, 28911 Leganés, Spain
{joseluis.martinez,paloma.martinez}@uc3m.es

Abstract. This position paper deals with queries beyond text, mixing several multimedia contents: audio, video, image and text. Search approaches combining some of these formats have been studied, including *query by example* techniques in situations where only one format is considered. It is worth mentioning that most of these research works do not deal with text content. A new approach to allow users introducing multimodal queries and exploring multimedia repositories is proposed. For this purpose, different ranked result lists must be combined to produce the final results shown for a given query. The main goal of this proposal is to reduce the semantic gap between low level features and high level concepts in multimedia contents. The use of qualitative data giving more relevance to text content along with machine learning methods to combine results of monomodal retrieval systems is proposed. Although it is too soon to show experimentation results, a prototype implementing the approach is under development and evaluation.

Keywords: multimodal queries, search engine, query by example, results lists combination, multimedia retrieval, relevance feedback.

1 Introduction

All Internet users have seen a growth of multimedia content available on the web. Services such as YouTube, Google Image, Flickr, Yahoo Video and others, have experienced an enormous development in the last few years. Besides, Google has recently announced a new product, Google TV[1], where online streaming videos will be part of the content offered to the user. On the other hand, traditional search engines

---

[*] This work has been partially supported by the Spanish Center for Industry Technological Development (CDTI, Ministry of Industry, Tourism and Trade), through the project Buscamedia (CEN-20091026). Authors would like to thank all Buscamedia partners for their knowledge and contribution.
[1] http://www.google.com/tv/

F. Alvarez and C. Costa (Eds.): UCMEDIA 2010, LNICST 60, pp. 35–40, 2012.
© Institute for Computer Sciences, Social Informatics and Telecommunications Engineering 2012

have evolved to deal with multimedia resources although, at the time of writing, it is not possible to use an image or a video in a query in any of these services. They are based on a manual or semi-automatic content tagging, but no content based retrieval seems to be applied. The work presented in this paper defines an approach to fill this gap, in order to consider queries containing text and/or audio and/or video and/or images, i.e., multimodal queries [13].

Let's suppose a scenario where the user has more data to express a query than some words. Suppose you have an MP3 file of a song and the name of one of the singers but you want to know the title of the song. Or imagine that you have a film in AVI format, a photo of the film director and you want to obtain his name to look for his filmography and the links to trailers of those films, if available. In this context, somehow related multimodal data is being used to represent a query and not only text should be retrieved but also audio, video and image contents, or even combinations of them. Some works like [13],[5],[10] have considered multimodal queries, pointing out the fact that only in recent years the information retrieval community is moving from dealing with one media at a time to combining more than one media in a retrieval process. In contrast, if some of this research is studied in detail, it is possible to see that the term multimedia usually excludes textual content or it refers to metadata related to the content. There is no a real mix among documents, web pages, videos, images and audio files.

2   Accessing Multimedia Sources with Multimodal Queries

If Information Retrieval Systems are considered, there is a semantic gap between content representations stored in indexes and concepts represented by those contents. The main objective is to find the theme or subject of a content which could be referenced in a query. But there is an issue that cannot be left aside, the theme or subject must be specified from the point of view of the searcher. For example, in a picture of happy children playing with a ball in the shore with a blue sea at the background, some searchers can be interested in finding photos with blue background and some others could be interested in photos where smiling children appear. Of course, this would be the ideal behavior of a multimedia retrieval system. In practice, it is not still possible to take into account every facet of some content in order to support any user need. For the moment, specific domain and restricted applications can be carried out with acceptable results, as demonstrated by evaluation forums such as TREC[2] or CLEF[3].

In order to deal with the semantic content of multimedia data, different abstraction levels are adopted [8][6]. The first one is formed by low level features, such as color, texture, shape and others for images; motion and direction, among others, for video; tone, spectral rile off or energy entropy for audio; and words, lemmas or n-grams for text. The second abstraction level is constituted by semantic representations of the contents, which are obtained by processing low level features and group together all

---

[2] http://trec.nist.gov
[3] http://www.clef-campaign.org

contents referring to some concept. Finally, there is a third level where intelligent reasoning is considered to infer some new knowledge from the semantic content; as an example, if some content is related with the semantic concept *smile*, then it can be part of a query related to *happiness*.

Although some of the previous research works deal with more than one format for the data, ([6] considers audio and video features to index the collection, [7], [11] deals with images and texts) it is difficult to find initiatives where a combination of formats is used to define a query. Most of the research works on multimedia information fusion deal with classifiers and combinations of them in different ways. [3] describes a combination of linear classifiers in order to reinforce semantics in the retrieval process. [2] successfully applies heterogeneous late fusion of independent retrieval models to retrieve data from a collection of annotated images.

Some evaluation tasks where queries are specified through text and image are defined in [7], but it is not the common situation. On the other hand, commercial search engines do not allow using other than text to define a query nor a combination of text, video, image and audio.

2.1   An Approach to Multimodal Retrieval

This section describes an innovative approach proposed in this research work to process multimodal queries in multimedia environments, see Fig. 1. The aim is to perform different search processes, in a somehow independent way, mixing obtained results for each process in a unique ranked list. The process to mix partial result lists is driven by semantics, which is obtained from all available formats (shapes recognition in images, concepts detection in video [6], etc.)

According to [9] the data fusion taken into account in this proposal could be considered into the ranking level model category, where several ranked streams are used to produce a consensus ranking, but also into the decision level model category, where the composing retrieval systems only provide a final decision (not a ranked list of probable results).

Seven different modules can be distinguished, which are described below:

- *Query by example*: This block includes common query by example techniques for each media. For media contents other than text, these algorithms will find similar contents for the different media, obtaining one result list for each. In the case of audio indexing, *query by humming* is also considered. Text queries consisting on a complete document would go through this path.
- *Text Search*: It covers all issues related to text based queries including: *free text* queries, formed by some words; *question answering*, providing accurate answers to questions; and *metadata queries*, asking about structured data defined in a semantic resource, including ontologies. The final goal is to provide relevant results for any kind of text-based search expression written by a user, but applying the right text search procedures depending on the content and structure of the query. A unique result list is obtained as a response to a text-based query.

- *Media Indexing*: Techniques for content-based indexing of image, audio and video data are part of this piece. [1] and [8] describe some of the methods to build indexes for each type of media. The output for this module is formed by three indexes, one for video, one for audio and another one for image contents.

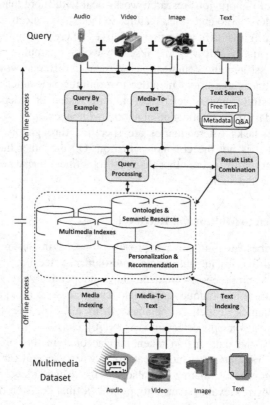

Fig. 1. Graphical representation of the proposed approach to multimodal query expression and retrieval

- *Text Indexing*: It covers all issues related to text based information retrieval, including the ability to provide semantic annotations for texts, employing semantic resources such as ontologies, thesaurus and so on. The output is a text index that will be used by the text search process.
- *Media-To-Text*: This module is in charge of obtaining textual representations for media contents, to make possible a text search process using these transformations. Of course, depending on the type of media, specific transformation methods are applied. Some of these methods have been described in [8]. Some of them have low quality ratios (as an example, only 60%-70% of the words are correctly recognized by ASR systems) which will be transmitted along the proposed retrieval process. One of the goals of this research work is to apply natural language processing tools as well as semantic web resources, such as ontologies, to reduce the effect of transformation errors.

- *Query Processing*: The right combination of the different media provided in the query is a key issue before running information retrieval processes on isolated media. For example, the following situations should be distinguished: if a given text must be found on an audio transcript or if it is the title of an audio file.
- *Results list combination*: According to previous component descriptions, several retrieval results lists are obtained, depending on the media used to represent the query. This final module is in charge of producing a unique result list, either using elements of different lists to build an entry for the final list or merging partial results lists in a final list or both. This module can also take into account ranking conditions, in order to pay more attention to results coming from one list or from another (for example, in some situations results coming from the video retrieval list could be more relevant than those coming from the text-based one). It is also possible to take into account personalization and recommendation data to consider users' preferences and information about previous experiences and interactions with other users. There exist a huge previous research work in the area, as can be read in [4] and [12].

3   Future Work

This paper identifies a shortage in current multimedia retrieval methods: it is difficult to find approaches dealing with all media: text, audio, video and image. Most of the previous research work seems coming from the video and audio retrieval communities and, if text is considered, it is supposed to come from transcripts or OCR processes. For this reason, a framework to consider all types of media is defined, based on the combination of partial result lists obtained by retrieval processes on isolated media. Besides, if multimodal queries are provided, the ability to integrate the different formats in queries on isolated media is also taken into account; semantic resources are applied for this purpose.

Of course, there is a lot of work to do, an initial implementation of the approach is under development, which must be tested under somehow standard evaluation frameworks, such as the ones developed in TREC or CLEF forums.

References

1. Bashir, F.I., Khanvilkar, S., Schonfeld, D., Khokhar, A.: Multimedia Systems: Content Based Indexing and Retrieval. In: Chen, W. (ed.) The Electrical Engineering Handbook, sec. 4, ch. 6. Academic Press (2004)
2. Escalante, H.J., Hérnandez, C.A., Sucar, L.E., Montes, M.: Late fusion of heterogeneous methods for multimedia image retrieval. In: Proceeding of the 1st ACM International Conference on Multimedia information Retrieval, MIR 2008, Vancouver, British Columbia, Canada, October 30-31, pp. 172–179. ACM, New York (2008)
3. Joshi, D., Naphade, M., Natsev, A.: Semantics reinforcement and fusion learning for multimedia streams. In: Proceedings of the 6th ACM International Conference on Image and Video Retrieval, CIVR 2007, Amsterdam, The Netherlands, July 09-11, pp. 309–316. ACM, New York (2007)

4. Martínez-Santiago, F.: El problema de la fusión de colecciones en la recuperación de información multilingüe y distribuida: cálculo de la relevancia documental en dos pasos. Doctoral Thesis, UNED (2004)
5. Mittal, A.: An Overview of Multimedia Content-Based Retrieval Strategies, Informatica. International Journal of Computing and Informatics 30(3), 347–356 (2006)
6. Naphade, M.R., Kristjansson, T., Frey, B., Huang, T.S.: Probabilistic Multimedia Objects Multijects: A novel Approach to Indexing and Retrieval in Multimedia Systems. In: Proc. IEEE International Conference on Image Processing, vol. 3, pp. 536–540 (1998)
7. Nowak, S., Dunker, P.: Overview of the CLEF 2009 Large-Scale Visual Concept Detection and Annotation Task. In: Peters, C., Caputo, B., Gonzalo, J., Jones, G.J.F., Kalpathy-Cramer, J., Müller, H., Tsikrika, T. (eds.) CLEF 2009. LNCS, vol. 6242, pp. 94–109. Springer, Heidelberg (2010),
http://www.clef-campaign.org/2009/working_notes/Overview_VCDT.pdf
8. PetaMedia: State of the art report. PetaMedia Deliverable D 5.1 (2008)
9. Poh, N., Kittler, J.: Multimodal Information Fusion, Multimodal Signal Processing: Theory and Applications for Human-Computer Interaction. In: Thiran, J.-P., Bourlard, H., Marques, F. (eds.) to appear in Elsevier Science (2009) ISBN-13: 978-0-12-374825-6
10. Olsson, J.S., Oard, D.W.: Combining Speech Retrieval Results with Generalized Additive Models. In: Proceedings of ACL 2008: HLT, Association for Computational Linguistics, pp. 461–469 (2008)
11. Tollari, S., Detyniecki, M., Marsala, C., Fakeri-Tabrizi, A., Amini, M., Gallinari, P.: Exploiting Visual Concepts to Improve Text-Based Image Retrieval. In: Boughanem, M., Berrut, C., Mothe, J., Soule-Dupuy, C. (eds.) ECIR 2009. LNCS, vol. 5478, pp. 701–705. Springer, Heidelberg (2009)
12. Wiguna, W., Fernández-Tébar, J., García-Serrano, A.: Using a Fuzzy Model for Combining Search Results from Different Information Sources to Build a Metasearch Engine. In: Computational Intelligence, Theory and Applications, pp. 325–334 (2006), doi:10.1007/3-540-34783-6_34
13. Yan, R.: Probabilistic Models for Combining Diverse Knowledge Sources in Multimedia Retrieval. PhD thesis, Carnegie Mellon University (2006)

KnoWhere: User's Attitudes towards and Experiences with an Experimental Location Based Service

Roland Craigie, Doug Williams, and Stephen Johnson

BT Innovation and Design, Adastral Park, Ipswich, UK., IP5 3RE
{roland.craigie,doug.williams,stephen.h.johnson}@bt.com

Abstract. Users' attitudes towards the use of an experimental location based service running on a mobile phone using Wi-Fi beacons as a locator are reported. Twenty one users took part in the trial and sixteen went on to be active users. Detailed results based on logging and user interviews are reported exploring usage, perceptions and experiences. The attitudes reported to a service of this type were generally positive.

Keywords: location based services. Wi-Fi, mobile.

1   Introduction

Context enriched services are recognised as a key growth area for mobile based services [Jones, 2010], and these are expected to emerge from the simple and ubiquitous location based services enabled by the fact that all mobile phones are able to offer some level of location information, using cellular, Wi-Fi or satellite technologies. In parallel there is a growing interest in understanding how to offer services that work with users' social networks, providing services that augment or depend upon services such as Facebook[1]. This work explores user's attitudes towards a prototype location application, called KnoWhere. KnoWhere is a mobile phone application that automatically shares a small amount of information about your geographic location. In this work we have investigated the use of, and attitudes towards this application, when used between a group of self selected close friends, colleagues or family members in trials that lasted up to ten weeks. KnoWhere is not an overtly commercial advertising or incentive based application; rather it invites users to gain comfort and utility from knowing the location of close friends.

Participants' use of the application was monitored through logs and their attitudes towards it were recorded through interviews and questionnaires. Twenty one people were engaged in testing the application in six groups. The tests took place over a period of six months. The authors anticipated a degree of suspicion towards and wariness of the application, believing that users would feel uncomfortable using an application that revealed their location.

---

[1] Facebook (link checked May 2010) www.facebook.com

F. Alvarez and C. Costa (Eds.): UCMEDIA 2010, LNICST 60, pp. 41–50, 2012.
© Institute for Computer Sciences, Social Informatics and Telecommunications Engineering 2012

Not surprisingly, use of the application varied from user to user, but the log results tend to show that, for those that used the application, after an initial flurry of activity, usage tapered down to a residual constant level. In interviews no users reported feeling uncomfortable about the way the software recorded and published their location data. Five of the six groups reported a real or anticipated benefit from using the application. For some this benefit was based on the ability to better orchestrate specific events, like meeting a friend. For others it was a "warm feeling" of having an awareness of another's activity.

The main criticisms were related to the phone and not the application; users tended towards demanding more from the application, wanting more control and wanting it to reveal more rather than less about their location.

We conclude that, when designed to give users control over the way they reveal and tag locations, services that automatically reveal an individual's location could be popular with some users.

2   Background

Location based services are not new. A range of different technologies can be used to help ascertain location. Perhaps most successful is the Global Positioning System, the technology behind satellite navigation systems, which provides positioning information accurate to within a few metres calculated from the difference in time stamps received from (ideally) at least 4 visible satellites. GPS work best outside when there is an unobstructed view of the sky and hence the satellites.

For cell phones, cell ID can be used to provide some indication of position, though the accuracy of such systems will depend upon the separation of the mobile phone masts and the accuracy to which the location of a given mast is known. Chen et al. [Chen, M., et al., 2006] report a (best) median error of 94m based on tests in Seattle. In general, errors will vary from a few tens of metres to a few kilometers.

Locating based on proximity to the known locations of Wi-Fi access points can give an accuracy of a few tens of metres [LaMarca et al. 2005]. Here, the access point locations are determined by a process known as wardriving (searching for Wi-Fi access points in a car and cross correlating the WI-Fi identifiers with a known GPS location). While the database coverage of such systems in urban areas is now very good, rural areas still lack both Wi-Fi availability and the database mapping, and as a result, this approach will not provide universal positioning.

Services such a Google's Latitude and in car navigation systems often use a hybrid positioning approach where the position is derived primarily from GPS but also, in instances when the GPS signal may be weak or absent, through other means such as Wi-Fi or Cell ID positioning, or using dead reckoning to extrapolate your position in a moving vehicle based on a knowledge of your last know location, trajectory and your speed.

These technologies are used in the provision of location based services that allow users to share their location with the world or with their friends through commercial services such as FourSquare[2], Brightkite[3], Latitude[4] (from Google), and experimental applications such as Locaccino[5] and Locyoution [Tsai et al., 2009].

Brightkite, Locaccino and Locyoution all emphasise the social networking aspects of the service. Brightkite allows users to post a message along with their location (which provides some context to accompany the location information). Locaccino and Locyoution are Facebook applications and are thus implicitly linked with social networking. FourSquare has a business model based around advertising and enables commercial premises to make incentivized offers to individuals using their location. Alternatively Skyhook[6] makes available a location engine which can provide location information for use in other applications or devices.

Experimental research has been published on location based services. This includes assessments of concern about privacy [Barkhuus and Dey, 2003] and about methods for overcoming such issues [Toch et al., '09]. Locaccino, which is designed with knowledge of the perceived privacy concerns sets out to offer people tight control over the user groups with whom they share their information.

3   The KnoWhere Application

KnoWhere is a software application that runs on a mobile phone. KnoWhere uses Wi-Fi access points to identify locations and builds on previous work of Johnson, [Johnson, 2007]. The application allows users to tag particular locations with whatever name-label they like. In the naming process KnoWhere will offer up, as a possible location tag, the location scraped from the user's Microsoft Outlook calendar, though users can ignore or change this if they wish.

HTC 620   HTC 710   HTC HD2

Fig. 1. The phone types used within the trial were all variants of HTC windows mobile devices

---

[2] FourSquare (link tested May 2010) http://foursquare.com
[3] Brightkite (link tested May 2010) http://brightkite.com
[4] Latitude (link tested May 2010) www.google.com/latitude
[5] Locaccino (link tested May 2010) http://locaccino.org

Skyhook, (link tested May 2010):
[6] http://skyhookwireless.com

In normal operation, the application will wake up every 10 minutes (this periodicity can be changed), turn on the phone's Wi-Fi connectivity if it is not currently on and "sniff" for Wi-Fi access points. If the Wi-Fi fingerprint detected matches the fingerprint of a labeled Wi-Fi signature, then that label is published to a presence server. If the Wi-Fi signature is not recognized the user's location is published as 'unknown'. If no Wi-Fi connectivity is detected the location will be uploaded as "undefined".

The application was designed to minimize battery usage and so would automatically turn Wi-Fi off after its periodic "sniff". In our work the application worked with a range of HTC Windows mobile devices including the HTC 620, The HTC 710 and the HTC HD2 phone which are all shown in Figure 1.

The application presented a user's published location on the home screen of the phone so they could easily see, and if necessary adjust, the location they published to the presence server. The location of others could be seen by clicking on the KnoWhere application shown on the home screen. This action polled the KnoWhere presence server and presented the results as a simple textual table.

KnoWhere was designed for use by closed user groups and is targeted in our trials at groups of close friends or family members.

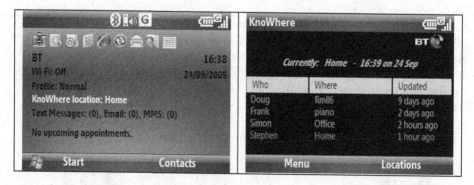

Fig. 2. The mobile phone home screen (which shows the location the user was publishing) and the KnoWhere page, which displays the locations of the user's close friends/family

4   Experimental

In order to learn more about a sample of potential users' attitudes to, and use of the KnoWhere application, we conducted a number of user trials in which groups of people were invited to use the KnoWhere application for between six and fourteen weeks. A condition for participation was that users must use one of the eligible HTC smart phones as their main phone for the duration of the trial. We had available four HTC 620s and two HTC 710 variants.

The application either came pre-loaded on the loan phones, or could be downloaded and installed on the phone by the users. Clear written and verbal instructions were offered as was personal help in order to get the application up and running. Once the trial had started the researchers made no interventions unless they suspected from log results that there had been a system malfunction.

Usage was recorded in logs, which were triggered every time users activated the KnoWhere application on the phone or tagged a new location. At the end of the trial users were invited to take part in a short on-line questionnaire and to take part in a closing interview.

When the phone scanned its environment in order to create a location tag, a local log was stored on the phone. By default, the scanning periodicity was 10 minutes though this was a user adjustable setting. When the phone had stored 20 instances of such scans (if there was a data plan in place) it attempted to upload this file to the server, for which it needed some kind of data connection either Wi-Fi or GPRS. If no data plan was in place the data remained on the phone and was collected at the end of the trial.

Data costs users incurred through using the application were covered by the research budget and at the end of the trial the user returned the loan phones.

The data collected included a user ID, the time, the tag name and whether the application had been accessed. This data allowed us to build pictures of the number of tags that people identified, the names they gave the tags and the number of times the application was accessed by the user. Together these enabled us to develop a picture of the usage by each individual.

Towards the end of the trial users were invited to fill in a simple form based on nine statements/questions. Eight of these were multiple choices, the ninth asked for a free text response.

Armed with the questionnaire responses we invited the trialists to take part in short interviews. These allowed us to go over the answers to the on-line questionnaire and to receive more elaborate and qualitative feedback. The interviews lasted about 30 minutes and where possible were held with as many members of the groups as possible in order to elicit more qualitative data on how such location based systems could serve the needs of groups.

5   Results

The trial took place in three phases because of the limited availability of the loan phones. The initial recruiting email was sent to about 150 people; this ultimately yielded six user groups including 11 people from the company. Other users were friends and family. The make-up of the groups is described in Table 1.

Table 1. Outline description of the six user groups

Group ID	No of participants	Constitution	Days persistent usage
G1	4	Mum, Dad, friend who helped with childcare, teenage boy	67, 70, 61, 53
G2	5	Group of friends	22, 18, 47, 2, 0
G3	4	Mum, Dad and late teenage daughter, son	141, 93, 98, 0
G4	4	Mum, Dad, daughter, son	5, 46, 2, 0
G5	2	Couple	40, 2
G6	2	Couple	57, 35

Number of activations of the KnoWhere application per day for each trialist

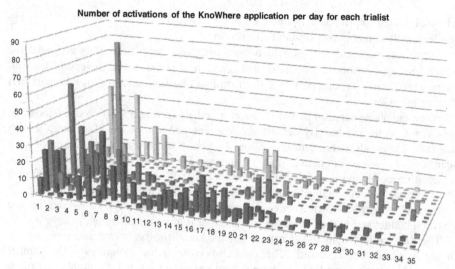

Fig. 3. The graph shows the number of daily activations of the KnoWhere application

A number of onerous practical complications had to be overcome during the set-up stage. One user for example whilst having a data plan in place, had a system that did not allow XMPP traffic used to communicate with the presence server and so their location data could not be transferred. This situation was eventually changed following communication with the service provider. Other issues including making sure that the phones were unlocked for the network used by each participant's service provider. Another hassle was negotiating the data plan (as far as possible) so that the cost of data traffic (primarily the log data only needed for the trial) could be covered by the research group. It was our intention that the triallists could take part in the trial at zero financial cost to themselves. All of these issues proved tractable but were time consuming.

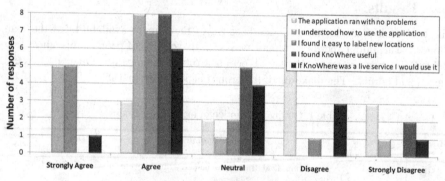

Fig. 4. On line questionnaire responses

Of the 21 triallists recruited only 15 became active beyond day 4 of their trial. Data were collected from these 15 triallists. The users tended to use the application more during the first few days but usage declined steadily towards the end of the trial.

Nevertheless users reported in interview, and the logs confirm, that usage continued at a low level with users checking the application "once or twice a week".

Questionnaire feedback forms were completed by 16 of the original 21 recruits and included one set of responses from a participant who was not active beyond day 4 of their trial. One questionnaire was substantially incomplete. The results from the on-line questionnaires are summarized below.

Users who persevered with the application for more than four days labelled between 3 and 28 different locations each. Overall 128 different name labels were recorded. Some tags were common such as 'Home'. The mean number of tags identified was about 8.5 and the mode was between 4 and 6.

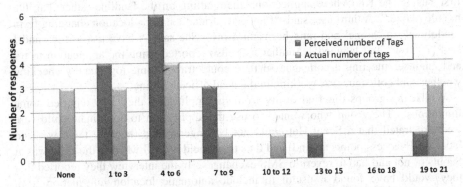

Fig. 5. The number of labels created (actuals and user reported)

Location tags included address-like titles such as a town name, building name, shop name, or room number, but also included descriptions which would mean little to someone who was not a member of the group, such as Gym, Nana's, Town or Hair. As reported elsewhere [Barkhaus et al., 2008] some of the labels were deliberately playful including affectionate names for users' homes and labels such as 'not running'.

Interviews were conducted with 10 of the 15 active users. In the interview users described choosing labels with a particular audience in mind. One user said "I chose labels that <child's name> would understand". The same user also identified not only that they were in a coffee area at work, but which side of that room they were in; this made chance meetings over lunch or a cup of coffee more likely.

The most common frequency of checking the application (measured over the last fourteen days of each user's trial) was between 1 and 3 times per day.

6   Discussion

As with many trials of this type, it was not easy to recruit users. The reasons for this were often related to user's reluctance to change their mobile phone. The phone and its behaviour were also the cause of criticism within the trial; one user reported "For me the main problem was the battery life. It was significantly shorter <than my old

phone.>". Whilst relevant overall to the user experience these criticisms should not be associated with the application, which for the most part was accepted warmly and appreciated by the users.

Groups used the application to different extents and in different ways. One group, who were highly purposeful in the way they sought to use location information, wanted to use it to aid in the picking up and dropping off of a child for whom they all shared some child care responsibility. Others were less intentional in their use but found their behaviour changing in small ways because of the application. One of Group two commented: "<friend's name> lives next door to me. When going to visit him instead of calling I would check his location." And another user similarly reported "When calling <Friend> I found myself checking if her mobile was at home first <using the KnoWhere application> then calling on the landline rather than the mobile phone." A third user said: "I noticed <friend's name> location changing from 'undefined' to 'home' and rang her right away. She said "I have just got in" and I said "I know" and laughed." Another user also reported using the application to try and engineer meeting a colleague so they could travel home together by checking whether said colleague was working in the head office building.

Whilst the groups did find utility from the application they also reported some limitations. The group who wanted to use the application to coordinate child care were frustrated that a Scout Hut could not be fingerprinted (because there were no local Wi-Fi access points around) and thus they could not tell whether the child was at Scouts or not and had to revert to SMS exchanges. In the interview they reported that they would have found it useful to include automatic location information from sources such as Cell ID or even GPS as this would let them know when the child was waiting outside the scout hut. They also told us that imagined that "knowing <friend> was in North Ipswich would be useful; at least I would know they had left work and were on their way…".

One of the young professionals was a strong advocate of the system but was frustrated by the fact that so few of their friends were using the system "to really work I'd have to get all my friends on the system that would be really useful. I can imagine deciding to go to particular pub to meet up if I could see where most of my friends were that evening."

One triallist commented that whilst location information was interesting it had limited utility without a context. They felt it would be more useful if information, such as the duration for which a person had been in a particular location, had been included.

One user suggested that alarms or alerts could prompt the user when a person was in the same location as them or when a person had reached a particular location – this would prevent users having to continually monitor the system and provide the utility required.

The KnoWhere application only offered users one group to which they could belong. Users anticipated that they would like to be able to manage several groups and commented that they would like to manage the permissions for different people in different ways so that the same place might be visible in different ways. An office location say, may be labelled quite specifically for work colleagues, but just identified as 'work' for non-work colleagues for whom the specific address would be meaningless. Similarly they felt that location outside work hours or outside the work location should not be made visible to people in a work group. One user commented "I think there should be a way to create groups to configure this as I might not want all of my contacts to see my location at any time."

One user also suggested they would like an override function so that the user could change the location published by the system temporarily.

Applications such as KnoWhere, which have the potential to disclose information about an individual, in this case their location, can be viewed as raising significant privacy concerns. The authors anticipated these to be issues of some concern to our user group. However, no one mentioned privacy unless prompted. When prompted, users reported that they had no concerns. We interpret this as suggesting that our users were satisfied and comfortable with the notion that their location was being shared within their well understood and controlled friendship group. One user commented "provided that the information is being shard in the way that I have been told it is being shared it is not a concern."

7   Conclusions and Further Work

KnoWhere is a small software client which runs on a mobile device. KnoWhere automatically determines its location and shares it with your chosen peer group. KnoWhere uses Wi-Fi access points as its location points and allows users to each apply a personalised tag to any Wi-Fi enabled location; the device will then publish the tag whenever it returns there. This application provides the basis for a very simple consumer and a corporate whereabouts service that works well indoors unlike other technologies such as GPS.

The results from the study suggest that whilst the application was valued by consumers they would value it more if the coverage it offered was more complete. Value was recognised for practical intentional tasks, like arranging to meet people at a certain location, but also as a way of keeping people who know each other well connected and aware of each other when apart. This leads us to suggest that location based services could be targeted at close friends and families but for appropriate utility they should be based on multiple location technologies and not just Wi-Fi. Future research should be conducted into the impact of publishing greater contextual information about a person's location in order to provide users with a richer picture about the tracked person's intent and action.

The fact that users did not reveal high anxiety levels about privacy issues within the trial suggests to us that some people are happy for devices to automatically disclose information about their location to a group of people that they select.

Acknowledgements. The research leading to these results has received funding from the European Community's Seventh Framework Programme (FP7/2007-2013) under grant agreement no. ICT-2007-214793.

References

1. Jones, N.: Context-Enriched Services: From Reactive Location to Rich Anticipation. Gartner analyst report, May 17 (2010), ID: G00175559
2. Barkhuus, L., Dey, A.: Location Based Services for mobile Telephony: a study of users' privacy concerns. In: Proceedings of Interact 2003, pp. 709–712 (2003)
3. Chen, M.Y., Sohn, T., Chmelev, D., Haehnel, D., Hightower, J., Hughes, J., LaMarca, A., Potter, F., Smith, I., Varshavsky, A.: Practical Metropolitan-Scale Positioning for GSM Phones. In: Dourish, P., Friday, A. (eds.) UbiComp 2006. LNCS, vol. 4206, pp. 225–242. Springer, Heidelberg (2006)
4. LaMarca, A., Chawathe, Y., Consolvo, S., Hightower, J., Smith, I., Scott, J., Sohn, T., Howard, J., Hughes, J., Potter, F., Tabert, J., Powledge, P.S., Borriello, G., Schilit, B.N.: Place Lab: Device Positioning Using Radio Beacons in the Wild. In: Gellersen, H.-W., Want, R., Schmidt, A. (eds.) PERVASIVE 2005. LNCS, vol. 3468, pp. 116–133. Springer, Heidelberg (2005)
5. Tsai, J.Y., Kelley, P., Drielsma, P., Cranor, L.F., Hong, J., Sadeh, N.: Who's Viewed You? The Impact of Feedback in a Mobile Location-Sharing Application. In: Proceeding of the 27th International Conference on Human Factors in Computing Systems CHI 2009 (2009)
6. Barkhaus, L., Brown, B., Bell, M., Hall, M., Sherwood, S., Chalmers, M.: From Awareness to Repartee: Sharing Location within social groups. In: Proceedings CHI 2008 I am Here Where Are You?, pp. 497–506 (2008)
7. Toch, E., Ravichandran, R., Cranor, L., Drielsma, P., Hong, J., Kelley, P., Sadeh, N., Tsai, J.: Analyzing use of privacy policy attributes in a location sharing application. In: Proceedings of the 5th Symposium on Usable Privacy and Security, SOUPS 2009 (2009)
8. Johnson, S.: A Framework for Mobile context-aware applications. BT Technology Journal 25(2) (April 2007)

Towards a Comprehensive Definition of User Experience for 3D Content

Raquel Navarro-Prieto and Elena Parra

Barcelona Media-Innovation Center
Av. Diagonal 177, 9th floor, 08018 Barcelona
Raquel.Navarro@barcelonamedia.org

Abstract. New developments in the area of 3D content have highlighted the need for the 3D content user experience evaluation within different media such as television, cinema, mobile and games. The goal of this paper is to present a theoretical approach and some preliminary data that tries to address the lack of an agreed definition of user experience, tackling the need for methodological guidelines in measuring user experience with 3D content. We propose that a number of cognitive and emotional processes need to be taken into account in order to fully understand the user experience with this type of content. We present a preliminary study that provides evidence about the importance of memory and attentional processes in the measurement of the user experience with stereoscopic content.

Keywords: user experience, 3D content, Quality of Service, cognitive processes, attention, memory, experimental study.

1   Introduction

The assessment of the subjective user experience has become a critical part of audiovisual quality assessment. In recent years researchers have tried to capture some parts of the user experience through the concept of Quality of Experience (QoE).

QoE has been defined as a subjective measure of performance for a system [1]. It relies on human opinion and differs from quality of service (QoS). Within standardization bodies the topic of QoE has been included into standardization activities for the measurement of QoE on audiovisual content in general, and for specific delivery platforms.

A fine example of the work efforts on this subject is found in ETSI HF STF 354 (Specialist Task Force 354 within the Human Factors Group of ETSI), aimed at providing requirement guidelines for real-time multimedia services with a good QoE. The goal of this set of standards is to provide the basis for objective and subjective measures on user experience for given communication situations, such as video and multimedia communication, and live TV (in the PC or mobile) [2]. Nevertheless, new media formats and communication technologies are setting up new challenges that prove the need to go beyond QoE to a more complete definition of the use experience with innovative content, still not covered by existing guidelines.

F. Alvarez and C. Costa (Eds.): UCMEDIA 2010, LNICST 60, pp. 51–59, 2012.

In particular, new developments in the area of 3D content have highlighted the need for the 3D content user experience evaluation within different media such as television, cinema, mobile and games. We find evidence for the lack of agreement on how to assess the user experience from innovative content in the fact that while widely recognizing the need to understand the sense of immersion in a given content, there is no standard or consensus on what this sense of immersion means or how to measure it.

The goal of this paper is to present a theoretical approach and some preliminary data that tries to address this gap, tackling the need for methodological guidelines in measuring user experience with 3D content. As we describe in more detail in section 2, we propose that a number of cognitive and emotional processes need to be taken into account in order to fully understand the user experience with this type of content.

Research efforts especially within European funded research projects, have addressed and are currently investigating three main aspects related to the user experience from 3D content. First, several studies are focused on measuring perceptual aspects such as the assessment of perceived depth or image quality [3, 4, 5, 7, 16, 17, 18]. These studies have tried to go further than the general International Telecommunication Union (ITU) recommendations for the subjective assessment of stereoscopic television images [6].

A second group of studies is trying to find ways to prevent visual discomfort with 3D stereoscopic content including the effect from variables from the viewing context or from mobile devices [6], [8]. The third group of studies is focused on finding better ways to interact with 3D content [4].

Little attention has been paid to understanding the user experience as a whole, including the complex processes involved in the sense of presence. Recent studies are starting to investigate a wider view of the user experience including aspects of 3D presence. In order to have a complete definition for user experience, we consider fundamental to understand the cognitive processes involved.

In the following section we expand the theoretical framework we propose in order to bridge the gap between the latest technology developments in the area of 3D content and our knowledge on how to measure the impact of this content upon users. Next, in section 3 we present a pilot study conducted with stereoscopic content in order to gather evidence on the involvement of cognitive processes from our theoretical framework. We close this paper with several conclusions from our work, and we discuss the next steps we expect to conduct in this area.

2   Proposed Factors Impacting the User's Experience

In this section we will present several theoretical and methodological research questions that we propose should guide further work in order to investigate user experience with 3D content. In particular we will focus on how cognitive and emotional processes may be involved in the reception, interpretation and interaction with different types of 3D content under different viewing conditions.

2.1   Which Variables Impact User Experience of 2D Content?

As a starting point for understanding user experience with 3D content, we have reviewed which aspects have been shown to have an impact on the user experience with 2D content. In our review, we found many variables that have been manipulated in lab experiments where different types of 2D content have been presented. In order to organize the main results from previous research, we have created two main categories of studies depending if the focus of the research was the impact of the content per se (1st category) or the impact of user's characteristics (2nd category).

1. In the category of research on the impact on QoE of **media specific variables**, three major type of characteristics of the content have been studied:

    I. First, some authors have investigated the effect of showing to the users multimedia content with differences in the way it has been structured. A good example of this type of research is the manipulation of the number of cuts in the content presented to the users. It has been proven [10] that the increase in the number of cuts in a film increases the attention during the time that the user is viewing it, but decreases memory of the events that happen in the film. In addition, [9] investigated the impact of forms, directions, colors and rhythm in the emotional reactions of viewers. In this later case, the authors provide a methodological review about how all these aspects have been studied in many experiments. Some of the conclusions for his review are that the valence of the emotion is correlated with form and colour, while the arousal of the emotions often correlates with rhythm and motion. According to the author: "The result from the analysis of the relationship between the structural property of both audio and visual stimuli and emotion provides support for the theories based on the iconic relationship concept".

    II. Secondly, the manipulation of perceptual variables from the viewing situation has been also shown to have an impact in user's emotions and memory. In particular, it is important not only whether the content is presented in 2D versus 3D in their central focus of attention but also if they are presented with 2D or 3D content in their peripheral vision [14]. Researchers have concluded that an hybrid condition were the users are presented a 3D image in between and overlapping onto two adjacent 2D images creates a higher sense of immersion than viewing the same content all in 3D. Another important effect is the impact of seating position and orientation regarding the screen in the subjective feeling of immersion. [13].

    III. Third, the impact of some intrinsic characteristic to the content like their emotional charge have been investigated showing that sensationalist news are remembered more than emotionally neutral news [10]. In addition, content if the content presented is real or fiction changes the memory and the emotions evoked by that content. [19].

    To summarize the main conclusions of the literature presented, we can conclude that the manipulation of the type of content and the viewing conditions have an important impact on several cognitive processes from perceptual, to attentional processes as well as memory and emotion [12].

2. The second category of variables that have been studied is the impact of user's personal characteristics on the user experience of a particular content. In particular, the individual variable that has been studied in many occasions is previous exposure to similar content [11], demonstrating that more attention is paid to new information. In addition, viewer's mood could decrease or increase how much they remember from the content [10].

To conclude, we claim that it is very important to integrate all these variables into a framework in order to understand the effects that may emerge from the interaction among all these aspects on spectators, and to test these effects with different types of media.

With the goal of creating such a framework, which will take information from the knowledge already accumulated with research on 2D content, we will discuss in the following subsections two challenges to which we have to pay attention in future research.

2.2 The Importance of a Investigating the Impact of the Variables across Different Types of Content and Contexts

The first aspect that we consider that has not been properly addressed in previous research is the validation of research results across contents and contexts. Up to now these variables have been investigated in the context of a very particular type of content, because they have been focused on answering very specific questions about the quality of particular media.

2.3 The Need to Validate an Appropriate Methodology

The second challenge in order to create a framework for 3D user experience is to be able to investigate how relevant are the factors that have proven to be important for 2D content for immersive media.

When facing this challenge, we encountered the need for a holistic definition for user experience that will allow us to understand which information to gather from the users and therefore, how it needs to be gathered. This definition should go beyond the perceptual factors and include cognitive processes (i.e. memory and attention) as well as the emotional responses and social variables. As we have discussed in the introduction, a considerable amount of work has been focused on how to test the visual perceptual aspects for the quality of the images and amount of visual discomfort, but much less is known about how to objectively measure the degree of engagement and cognitive reactions to the content.

Therefore, the research community will need to focus on creating a corpus of recognized methodologies to measure the relevant variables involved. In our view, in order to reach this goal and a wide consensus on the definition of user experience, we required a multidisciplinary approach. Research from different perspectives will be complementary and will advance our knowledge in an iterative manner. For instance, a social science observational approach can contribute with laying down the hypothesis. This hypothesis will then be very valuable to a second collaborative step between technology developers and experimental researchers using cognitive psychology. Such an approach would allow testing the laid down hypotheses and setting new research questions in order to reach consented conclusions on what a holistic definition of user experience for 3D media should encompass. Furthermore, we believe this approach will allow going beyond a descriptive approach and predicting how to create media to optimize the users' response.

As part of this multidisciplinary effort, we consider very important to review the work done on Cognitive Psychology about the relevance of several cognitive processes in information processing in general [9]. After this review we can infer an initial hypothesis on the important cognitive processes to measure, attention and memory, and their relationship with the users' emotional reactions [10] in general, and in particular with new media. Indeed, reported research shows the impact of some media characteristic, such as the number of cuts, on memory and attention [11].

In line with this claim about the importance of cognitive processes to understand user experience, we have applied and extended several methodologies used in Cognitive Psychology to measure these processes. In section 3 we report our attempt to apply some of these methodologies to 3D content. To our knowledge, this would be first instance these methodologies have been used to measure user experience from 3D stereoscopic content.

3   Investigation the Impact of Cognitive Processes in User Experience with Stereoscopic Content

As discussed in the previous section, we consider it is important to investigate the involvement of cognitive and emotional processes in the user experience of stereoscopic content. Based on reported previous work, we conducted a trial to examine the impact of memory, attention and emotional reactions. A second goal in this study was to test how cognitive psychology methodologies can be successfully applied in a close to real projection environment. This experiment was conducted in collaboration with Doremi Technologies[1] in the frame of the project 2020 3D media[2]. The sampled users watched the content in an exhibition theater, so the conditions could be as close as possible to a real life environment. Fifteen adult subjects took part as the sample of users, 7 women and 8 men. s we wanted to gather the reactions of end users, None of them were experts in multimedia technologies or content production.

---

[1] www.doremilabs.com

[2] The goal of this project is to explore and develop novel technologies to support the acquisition, coding, editing, networked distribution, and display of stereoscopic and immersive audiovisual content providing novel forms of compelling entertainment at home or in public spaces. The users of the resulting technologies will be both media industry professionals as well as the general public. More information can be found at: www.20203dmedia.eu/

3.1   Material

In our study we used stereoscopic material created by DOREMI. A set of particular effects present in the stereoscopic material was agreed in order to test their impact:

- Blur effect, in particular motion blur, when the images edges get diffused more as the object moves more quickly.
- Out of screen effect, when an object in the scene gets out of the screen.
- 3D in general, or the effect of viewing the images in 3 dimensions.

In order to ascertain if there was an impact from the type of content, we categorized the content where the particular effects appeared according to two different variables:

- Emotional versus non-emotional content (i.e. an intrinsic characteristic of the content whether it has been created to evoke strong emotions or to inform).
- Real life versus fiction (i.e. whether is has been film or a synthetic produce image).

We chose and agreed to measure the two most relevant cognitive variables that we found important in previous studies with immersive material, namely, attention and memory.

3.2   Methodology

For our study, we measured attention and emotional reaction during the presentation of the content, and memory after the presentation. To measure **attention** we used a cognitive task, namely split-attention, which is widely employed as a standard method for this kind of processes. According to this methodology the user must occasionally perform a "secondary task" (in our case responding as quickly as possible to loud beeps) while performing what is called the "primary task" (in our case watching the stereoscopic material). The main assumption of this methodology is that the measured reaction time (and therefore the attention allocated) to the secondary task is directly related to the amount of attention given to the primary task [15].

Once they finished their viewing we checked their **memory** recall of the content through questionnaires addressing particular elements from the 3D content.

3.3   Results

Since we worked with a small sample of viewers we performed no statistical analysis. Nevertheless, we consider the qualitative analysis of our data is a valuable support to determine if our research merits further study or not.

i.   Results on Attention

In Graphic 1 below, we can observe that watching content with the out of screen (OOS) effect impacted users' attention. It can also be noticed that at the precise instant the OOS appears the reaction time to the secondary task (beeps) increases, confirming a higher level of attention to the 3D material (primary task).

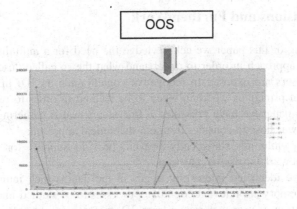

Fig. 1. Reaction time while watching the stereoscopic content

ii.   Results on Memory

We recorded the percentages of correctly answered questions. The results were divided depending on the content variables and the type of effect:

1. Content type; here we differentiate reality from animation sequences.
2. Type of effect; here we distinguish out of screen from 3D contents.

First, we detected a tendency in the results, which shows content with OOS effects (mean = 0.50; SD = 0.21) to be remembered better than the material with 3D effect (mean = 0.44; SD = 0.22), as illustrated on Figures 2. Second, as we can see in Figure 3, we found a trend favouring the recall of real content (mean = .046; SD = 0.19) compared to animated content (mean = 0.40; SD = 0.33).

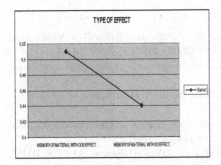
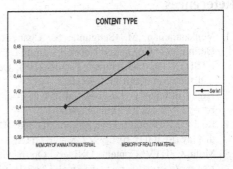

Fig. 2. and **3.** Comparison of remembrance between segments with out of screen effect and segments with 3D effects (left). Comparison of remembrance of real vs. animated material (right).

A hypothesis to be tested in future research is if the type of content has a direct effect on memory, and thus influences attention; which would mean both processes are involved in the feeling of immersion from the content.

4   Conclusions and Further Work

At the beginning of this paper we acknowledge the need for a multidisciplinary and comprehensive approach in order to understand what the so called "user experience" means, when users are exposed to innovative content such as 3D. In section 2 we highlight several principles we claim need to be studied in order to reach this goal. Later along the paper we have presented a first step towards gathering evidence on those variables we chose to consider from our theoretical approach.

Our results, while not statistically proven, provide support for the proposed theoretical framework in two main aspects:

First, we have identified interesting trends in the data, which indicate that both attention and memory are relevant cognitive processes to be studied in order to reach a holistic definition of user experience from 3D content. In our case, we found the OOS effect in the content increases both the attention and the remembrance over the watched piece of content.

In our ensuing work we would like to go one step further and record measurements related to the emotional state of the viewer [16], in order to test if a greater sense of immersion in the content is achieved when there is an increase of attention and memory recall.

Secondly, we have gathered some evidence on the outcomes from several effects in the content. In future studies we should consider presenting more controlled contents, where more so called Media Specific variables can be tested. In addition, we would like to use materials where the OOS effect is coupled with changes in other sensory areas such as hearing or touch, to test the effect of different sensorial inputs. In particular, we are preparing a study to investigate the effect of 3D audio.

References

1. Venkataraman, M., Sengupta, S., Chatterjee, M., Neogi, R.: Towards a Video QoE Definition in Converged Networks. In: ICDT 2007 (2007), ISBN: 0-7695-2910-0
2. ETSI TR 102 643, Human Factors (HF); Quality of Experience (QoE) requirements for real-time communication services
3. High Efficiency Laser-Based Multi-User Multi-Modal 3D Display, HELIUM3D, http://www.helium3d.eu/
4. Real 3D – Digital holography for 3D and 4D real-world objects' capture, processing, and display (Real3D), http://www.digitalholography.eu/
5. Mobile 3DTV Content Delivery Optimization over DVB-H System, Mobile 3DTV, http://sp.cs.tut.fi/mobile3dtv/
6. Rec ITU-R BT.1438, Subjective Assessment of Stereo- scopic Television Pictures
7. 3D Phone Project, http://www.the3dphone.eu
8. MacKay, D.G., Shafto, M., Taylor, J.K., Marian, D.E., Abrams, L., Dyer, J.R.: Relations between emotion, memory and attention: evidence from taboo stroop, lexical decision and immediate memory tasks. Memory Cognition 32(3), 474–488 (2004)
9. Somsaman, K.: Emotional expressiveness in visual-sonic integration: A framework for multimedia design. In: Proceedings CHI 2003, pp. 1024–1025 (2003)

10. Kubey, R., Csikszentmihalyi, M.: Scientific American mind. Televisión Addiction, 48–55 (2003)
11. Baños, R.M., Botella, C., Rubió, I., Quero, S., Garcia-Palacios, A., Alcañiz, M.: Presence and emotions in virtual environments: the influence of stereoscopy. CyberPsychology and Behavior 11(1), 1–8 (2008)
12. Prothero, J., Parker, D., Furner, T., Wells, M.: Towards a Robust, Quantitative Measure for Presence. In: Proceedings of the Conference on Experimental Analysis and Measurement of Situation Awareness, pp. 359–366 (1995)
13. Tasaki, S., Matsushita, T., Koshi, K., Wada, C., Koga, H.: Sense of Virtual Reality: Effectiveness of Replacing 3D Imagery with 2D/3D Hybrid Imagery. IEICE Transactions 88-D(5), 851–858 (2005)
14. Lang, A.: The limited capacity model of mediated message processing. The Journal of Communication 50(1), 46–70 (2000)
15. Blonch, S., Lemeignan, M.: Precise respiratory- posturo- facial patterns are realated to specific Basic emotions. Bewegen and Hulpverlening (1992)
16. Häkkinen, J., Kawai, T., Takatalo, J., Mitsuya, R., Nyman, G.: What do people look at when they watch stereoscopic movies? In: S&T/SPIE's International Symposium on Electronic Imaging: Science and Technology. Stereoscopic Displays and Applications XXI, San Jose, California, USA, January 18-21, vol. 7524 (2010)
17. Campisi, P., Benoit, A., Le Callet, P., Cousseau, R.: Quality assessment of stereoscopic images. Eurasip Journal on Image and Video Processing 2008 (2008)
18. Chen, W., Fournier, J., Barkowsky, M., La Callet, P.: New requirements of subjective video quality assessment methodologies for 3DTV. In: Video Processing and Quality Metrics 2010 (VPQM), Scottsdale, United States (2010)
19. Mendelson, A.L., Papacharissi, Z.: Realilty vs Fiction How Defined Realness Affects Cognitive & Emotional Responses to Photographs. Visual Communication Quarterly 14(4), 231–243 (2007)

Assessing the Effects of Ambient Illumination Change in Usage Environment on 3D Video Perception for User Centric Media Access and Consumption[*]

Gokce Nur, Safak Dogan, Hemantha Kodikara Arachchi, and Ahmet M. Kondoz

I-Lab Multimedia Communications Research, Faculty of Engineering & Physical Sciences,
Centre for Vision, Speech, and Signal Processing,
University of Surrey, Guildford GU2 7XH, Surrey, UK
{G.Nur,S.Dogan,H.Kodikaraarachchi,A.Kondoz}@surrey.ac.uk

Abstract. For enjoying 3D video to its full extent, access and consumption of 3D content should be user centric, which in turn ensures enhanced quality of user experience. The experience nevertheless is easily influenced by several factors, including content characteristics, users' preferences, contexts prevailing in various usage environments, etc. Utilizing ambient illumination as an environmental context for the purposes of efficient provision of 3D video to users has particularly not been studied in literature in detail. This paper investigates the effects of ambient illumination on 3D video quality and depth perception for utilizing this information as one of the key context elements in future user centric 3D access and consumption environments. Subjective tests conducted under different illumination conditions demonstrate that the illumination of the viewing environment encircling the users has significant effects on the perceived 3D video quality as well as depth perception.

Keywords: User centric 3D video, ambient illumination, usage environment, subjective quality assessment.

1 Introduction

Content distribution and access in heterogeneous usage environments have posed significant research and technology development challenges for delivering media to a wide range of users for a long time. These challenges have been exacerbated not only by the existence of different networking infrastructures, diverse user terminals, and numerous media content representations, but also by the users themselves and their various preferences and high levels of expectations. In turn, this has led the research efforts to focus on user centricity while providing media services rather than conventional purely technology oriented service provisions.

User centricity in media services is an all-encompassing concept, in which complying with regulations, standards, technological requirements, etc as well as decoupling such technologies from the users and making them as seamless and easy-to-use as possible are all inherently essential. While addressing all of these,

---

[*] This paper won the Best Paper Award of the UCMEDIA 2010 Conference.

F. Alvarez and C. Costa (Eds.): UCMEDIA 2010, LNICST 60, pp. 60–68, 2012.

responding to the user needs, requests and preferences while also paying attention to the usage environment conditions are certainly a major part of providing user centric media services successfully.

In recent years, users have increasingly become producers of large quantities of media content in addition to their traditional consumer roles, and thus a new term: *"prosumers"* has been coined to reflect the changing roles of the users. Consequently, this has resulted in an explosion of user generated content exchanged and distributed across the Internet. The media content, either user generated or created by professionals, is abundant and readily available for the consumption of a wide variety of users. Today's Internet access makes the content sharing and exchange possible, yet Future Media Internet will allow a wide range of new applications to be realized with support for ubiquitous media-rich content service technologies. 3D video is one of them, and has already made its way to becoming a world-wide success story.

The stereoscopic viewing ability of humans has always been the driving force behind the efforts for bringing 3D video technologies to reality. 3D video capture, representation, coding, transmission, rendering, etc are some example technologies to name [1]. Although several developments in these technologies have been made today, there are still many areas that need to be improved through vigorous research. For enjoying the 3D video to its full extent, access and consumption of 3D content should be user centric, which in turn ensures enhanced quality of user experience. Thus, user centric 3D video adaptation is one of the key areas that requires in-depth investigations for enabling next generation networked and pervasive 3D media environments, which will be available over the Future Media Internet.

The overall target of the user centric 3D video adaptation is to maximize user experience in terms of perceived quality and depth perception [2]. Hence, as a first step, it is necessary to determine the contextual factors that can affect the 3D video quality and depth perception during its consumption, so as to assist adaptation and efficient provision of 3D video to users for achieving this target. Particularly, the effects of varying ambient illumination context in the content usage environment surrounding the user on the use and experience of 3D video have not been thoroughly investigated in literature. In this paper, these effects are studied, assessed, and a set of notable findings is clearly highlighted. Based on the subjective tests employed involving a group of viewers, changes in the illumination conditions have been observed to affect users' quality of 3D video content viewing and consumption experiences. The knowledge gained through this assessment work is envisaged to be valuable for exploiting in developing user centric 3D video adaptation strategies, which will lead the path to successful provision of 3D video to users with various requirements and preferences.

Contextual data for ambient illumination can be gathered through light sensors placed on user devices, which collect information on the level of brightness in a consumption environment. Color-plus-depth map 3D video representation is employed for the research carried out in the paper since it has many advantages compared to the left and right 3D video representation, and has also been highly exploited in research and standardization activities to date [1] [3].

This paper is organized as follows. The subjective assessment test method is described in Section 2. Section 3 presents the results of the assessments, elaborates on them, and outlines a number of suggestions for exploiting the observations made from the analysis of the results. Finally, Section 4 presents the conclusions and future work.

2   Subjective Assessment Tests

In this section, the details of the test set-up and methodology followed to conduct the subjective experiments for assessing the video quality and depth perception during the user centric access and consumption of a range of 3D video sequences under different ambient illumination conditions in the usage environment are described.

In the experiments, a 42" Philips multi-view auto-stereoscopic display, which has a resolution of 1920 × 1080 pixels, was used to display six 3D video test sequences that are called as: *Interview*, *Chess*, *Windmill*, *Ice*, *Advertisement*, and *Eagle*. The thumbnails of these sequences are depicted in Fig. 1. The color texture and depth map sequences of the 3D video clips were of High Definition (HD) resolution (i.e., 1920 × 1080 pixels) at 25 fps. The Joint Scalable Video Model (JSVM) reference software version 9.13.1 was used to encode the sequences [4]. Four different channel bandwidths (i.e., 512, 768, 1024, and 1536 kbps) were selected as target bit rates. 80% of the target bit rate was allocated for the color sequences and the remaining bit rate (i.e., 20%) was allocated for the depth map sequences while performing the experiments [5]. The lengths of the videos were set to 5 seconds, which complies with the International Telecommunication Union (ITU)'s recommendation for subjective quality assessment experiments [6].

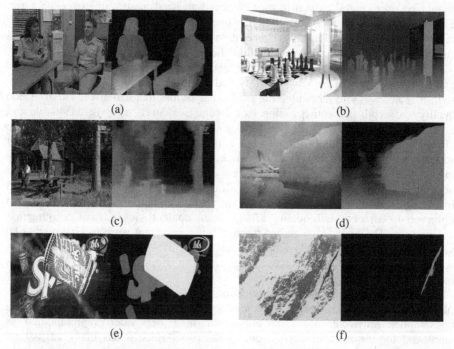

(a)   (b)

(c)   (d)

(e)   (f)

Fig. 1. Color texture and associated depth map of the (a) *Interview* (b) *Chess* (c) *Windmill* (d) *Ice* (e) *Advertisement* (f) *Eagle* sequences

The effects of the ambient illumination on perceptual quality and depth perception were assessed under four different ambient illumination conditions (i.e., 5, 52, 116, and 192 lux), created by the self-contained media laboratory facilities of I-Lab,

University of Surrey. 5 lux corresponds to a dark condition, while 192 lux indicates a bright light environment. These conditions were measured using a Gretag Macbeth Eye-One Display 2 device [7]. 16 volunteers (5 females and 11 males) participated in the experiments. They were all non-expert viewers, whose ages ranged from 20 to 35. Their eye acuity was tested against Snellen eye chart and the stereo vision was tested with the TNO stereo test. All of them surpassed 0.7 eye acuity and 60 seconds of arc stereo vision levels, respectively. Furthermore, their color vision was verified with the Ishihara test, and all viewers were reported to have good color vision [1]. The subjective tests were conducted with each viewer to assess all of the test sequences individually, which were randomly ordered for each environment condition to avoid any potential prejudices. The subjects were asked to assess both the video quality and depth perception by comparing the impaired video sequences with the reference ones. Following the experiments, the Mean Opinion Scores (MOSs) [6] obtained from all of the viewers were computed. A score of 5 in the MOS assessment scale means the impaired video has the same perceptual quality or depth perception as the reference one, while a score of 1 means very annoying presentation. The tests lasted 20 minutes on average, including the initial training session.

3 Results and Elaboration on Observations

In this section, the results of the subjective experiments are analyzed for the six test sequences in detail firstly. Subsequently, observations on the results are elaborated, and the application areas, in which such observations can be exploited, are discussed.

3.1 Results and Discussion

Figs. 2-4 illustrate the bit rate versus MOS results reported on the viewers' video quality and depth perception assessments for the 3D *Interview*, *Chess*, and *Windmill* sequences, respectively. It can be observed from the video quality results presented on the left-hand side graphs (i.e., the (a) figures) that the video sequences viewed under different ambient illumination conditions have demonstrated an increasing perceptual quality rating pattern as the amount of light in the environment increases across all of the bit rate range that was considered in the experiments. Here, the perceived video quality presents the lowest subjective scores in the 5 lux environment compared to those in the other environments regardless of the varying bit rate. When the ambient illumination increases (i.e., from 5 lux to 52 lux; to 116 lux; and to 192 lux), the subjective scores given by the viewers also increase. This is due to the fact that the size of the iris responds to the amount of ambient light entering into the eye, which directly influences the sensitivity of the Human Visual System (HVS) towards perceiving finer details in the visual content [8]. It is therefore no surprise that in the 5 lux (i.e., dark) environment, the HVS becomes more sensitive to detecting quality related problems while watching a video clip due to enlarged iris. In such an environment, the compression artifacts in the 3D visual scene are more visible to the eye than in the other environments. Thus, when the amount of ambient illumination in the consumption environment increases, the corresponding sensitivity of the HVS decreases due to reducing iris size, which allows for adjusting to more ambient light entering into the eye. As a result, the compression artifacts start becoming less and less distinguishable to the viewers' eyes.

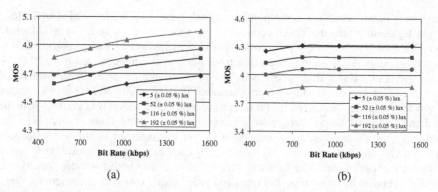

Fig. 2. The *Interview* sequence bit rate versus MOS under different ambient illumination conditions (5, 52, 116, and 192 lux) for (a) video quality (b) depth perception

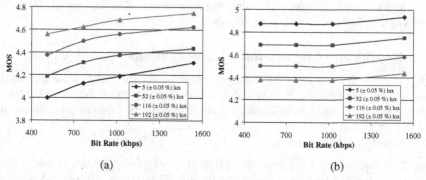

Fig. 3. The *Chess* sequence bit rate versus MOS under different ambient illumination conditions (5, 52, 116, and 192 lux) for (a) video quality (b) depth perception

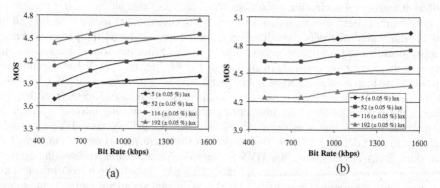

Fig. 4. The *Windmill* sequence bit rate versus MOS under different ambient illumination conditions (5, 52, 116, and 192 lux) for (a) video quality (b) depth perception

Interestingly, as can be observed from the depth perception results presented on the right-hand side graphs (i.e., the (b) figures), the video sequences viewed under different ambient illumination conditions have demonstrated a decreasing depth perception rating pattern as the amount of light in the environment increases across all of the bit rate range. Indeed, the perceived depth presents the highest subjective scores in the 5 lux environment when compared with those in the other environments regardless of the varying bit rate. When the ambient illumination increases (i.e., from 5 lux to 52 lux; to 116 lux; and to 192 lux), the subjective scores given by the viewers reduce. These results reveal that the lower the amount of ambient illumination in the 3D video access and consumption environment the better the depth perception MOS ratings are. This can be explained as follows: increased ambient illumination conditions do not necessarily contribute towards producing better 3D view effects to the HVS [9]. This is due to the fact that increased ambient illumination in the environment leads to reduced sensitivity to detecting sharpness, shadows, reflections, contrast differences, etc in the visual content, all of which are essential cues to enhance depth perception in 3D video. Although the depth related problems may be more eye-catching in a darker environment, as per the previous video quality discussions, the test results show that the viewers tend to overlook those impairments in the individual depth cues to favor the overall depth sensation received while watching 3D content in dark due to more prominent visibility of these cues [6, 10].

Furthermore, the experimental results have shown that as the encoding bit rates of the 3D video test sequences increase, both the perceived video quality and depth perception ratings improve. The improvement is larger for the video qualities for the increasing bit rate whereas there are several saturation levels in the depth perception results, observed with flat areas across the changing bit rate range. This is because, it is common knowledge that the compression quality of color texture visual content enhances with finer quantization in video coding, yet an increase in bit rate of depth maps does not reveal further depth information beyond what is already available.

Similar observations have been made on the video quality and depth perception results for the remaining 3D video test sequences, namely *Ice*, *Advertisement*, and *Eagle*. Due to space constraints in the paper, their individual bit rate versus MOS graphs have not been presented. Instead, the absolute MOS values obtained for the entire set of sequences are shown in Table 1, which support the observations reported.

3.2   Summary of Observations and Potential Exploitation of Knowledge Gained

The observations made during the experiments can be summarized as follows:

- When the ambient illumination in the usage environment for user centric 3D video access and consumption increases, the video quality perception ratings of the viewers also increase. The idea behind this observation is that in a well-lit environment, the visual artifacts (due to compression, transmission, rendering, etc) in the 3D content cannot be easily detected by the human eye as much as they can be noticed while viewing the same content in a dark environment.
- Conversely, when the ambient illumination in the environment increases, then the depth perception ratings of the viewers decrease, as brighter light conditions hinder the clear visibility of the essential cues (e.g., sharpness, shadowing, reflection, contrast, etc) that enhance the overall depth sensation in 3D content.

- When the bit rate of the 3D video increases, the MOS ratings associated with the video quality increase sharply, while the depth perception MOSs are presenting a mix of both smooth regions and areas of gradual increase.

In future research, the above-listed observations on the video quality and depth perception results, which provide useful hints for exploiting the HVS sensitivity to 3D video perception, can be utilized for realizing the development of:

- 3D media quality of experience enhancement solutions.
- Improved 3D media transmission and communication systems.
- Tailored user centric 3D video adaptation strategies.
- Easy-to-use/deploy 3D display and customized 3D rendering technologies.
- Personalized user centric 3D media access and consumption environments.

Table 1. Subjective assessment results

3D Video	Ambient Illum. (lux)	Bit Rate (kbps)	MOS		3D Video	Ambient Illum. (lux)	Bit Rate (kbps)	MOS	
			Video Quality	Depth Perception				Video Quality	Depth Perception
Interview	5	512	4.500	4.250	Ice	5	512	3.562	4.625
		768	4.562	4.312			768	3.625	4.687
		1024	4.625	4.312			1024	3.687	4.687
		1536	4.687	4.312			1536	3.875	4.687
	52	512	4.625	4.125		52	512	3.687	4.500
		768	4.687	4.187			768	3.812	4.562
		1024	4.750	4.187			1024	3.937	4.562
		1536	4.812	4.187			1536	4.125	4.562
	116	512	4.687	4.000		116	512	3.875	4.437
		768	4.750	4.062			768	4.062	4.500
		1024	4.812	4.062			1024	4.187	4.500
		1536	4.875	4.062			1536	4.375	4.500
	192	512	4.812	3.812		192	512	4.125	4.375
		768	4.875	3.875			768	4.375	4.437
		1024	4.937	3.875			1024	4.562	4.437
		1536	5.000	3.875			1536	4.750	4.437
Chess	5	512	4.000	4.875	Advertisement	5	512	2.875	4.875
		768	4.125	4.875			768	3.062	4.875
		1024	4.187	4.875			1024	3.187	4.937
		1536	4.312	4.937			1536	3.312	4.937
	52	512	4.187	4.687		52	512	3.125	4.625
		768	4.312	4.687			768	3.312	4.625
		1024	4.375	4.687			1024	3.437	4.750
		1536	4.437	4.750			1536	3.625	4.750
	116	512	4.375	4.500		116	512	3.437	4.375
		768	4.500	4.500			768	3.625	4.437
		1024	4.562	4.500			1024	3.812	4.437
		1536	4.625	4.583			1536	3.937	4.437
	192	512	4.562	4.375		192	512	3.812	4.250
		768	4.625	4.375			768	4.062	4.250
		1024	4.687	4.375			1024	4.250	4.375
		1536	4.750	4.437			1536	4.500	4.375

Table 1. (*Continued*)

Windmill	5	512	3.687	4.812	*Eagle*	5	512	4.000	4.750
		768	3.875	4.812			768	4.187	4.812
		1024	3.937	4.875			1024	4.375	4.875
		1536	4.000	4.937			1536	4.437	4.937
	52	512	3.875	4.625		52	512	4.187	4.687
		768	4.062	4.625			768	4.250	4.750
		1024	4.187	4.687			1024	4.437	4.812
		1536	4.312	4.750			1536	4.562	4.812
	116	512	4.125	4.437		116	512	4.312	4.562
		768	4.312	4.437			768	4.375	4.562
		1024	4.437	4.500			1024	4.562	4.625
		1536	4.562	4.562			1536	4.687	4.625
	192	512	4.437	4.250		192	512	4.375	4.375
		768	4.562	4.250			768	4.437	4.437
		1024	4.687	4.312			1024	4.625	4.500
		1536	4.750	4.375			1536	4.812	4.562

4   Conclusions and Future Work

In this paper, the effects of ambient illumination in the usage environment on the perceptual video quality and depth perception of 3D video sequences for user centric 3D video access and consumption have been investigated. The results of the investigations have revealed that ambient illumination has significant effects on the perceptual video quality and depth perception. Based on the subjective tests conducted with a group of viewers, it has been observed that when the ambient illumination in the content access and consumption environment increases, the MOS ratings of the viewers for the perceived video quality also increase. Conversely, it has also been noted that when the ambient illumination increases, the perceived depth MOS ratings of the viewers decrease. These observations provide a notable set of findings for realizing an enhanced support for networked user centric 3D media access and consumption methods, and thus can be exploited in quite a wide range of areas. Our future work comprises developing smart 3D video adaptation strategies by utilizing the knowledge gained through the experiments discussed in this paper.

References

1. Hewage, C.T.E.R., Worrall, S.T., Dogan, S., Villette, S., Kondoz, A.M.: Quality Evaluation of Color Plus Depth Map-Based Stereoscopic Video. IEEE J. Select. Topics in Sig. Process.: Visual Media Quality Assessment 3(2), 304–318 (2009)
2. Kim, M.B., Nam, J., Baek, W., Son, J., Hong, J.: The Adaptation of 3D Stereoscopic Video in MPEG-21 DIA. Elsevier Sig. Process. Image Commun. J. Special Issue on Multimedia Adaptation 18(8), 685–697 (2003)
3. ISO/IEC JTC 1/SC 29/WG 11: Committee Draft of ISO/IEC 23002-3 Auxiliary Video Data Representations. WG 11 Doc. N8038 (April 2006)
4. JSVM 9.13.1: CVS Server, http://garcon.ient.rwth-aachen.de/cvs/jv

5. Tikanmaki, A., Gotchev, A., Smolic, A., Miller, K.: Quality Assessment of 3D Video in Rate Allocation Experiments. In: IEEE Symposium on Consumer Electronics (April 2008)

6. ITU-R BT.500-11: Methodology for the Subjective Assessment of the Quality of Television Pictures (2002)

7. Gretag Macbeth Eye-One Display 2, http://www.xrite.com

8. Frazor, R.A., Geisler, W.S.: Local Luminance and Contrast in Natural Images. Elsevier Vision Research J. 46(10), 1585–1598 (2006)

9. Robinson, T.R.: Light Intensity and Depth Perception. American J. Psychology 7(4), 518–532 (1896)

10. ITU-R BT.1438: Subjective Assessment of Stereoscopic Television Pictures (2000)

Emerging Research Directions on 3D Video Quality Assessment*

Jaroslaw Bułat, Michal Grega, Lucjan Janowski, Dawid Juszka,
Mikolaj Leszczuk, Zdzislaw Papir, and Piotr Romaniak

Department of Telecommunications,
AGH University of Science and Technology

Abstract. Motion picture producers, providers and equipment developers have to deeply consider end user perception of the application being often expressed in terms of a capacious Quality of Experience (QoE) concept. QoE is affected across the whole application delivery chain including content digitisation and compression, its network delivery and reproduction. During recent years enormous research effort and massive tests have been performed in order to identify factors affecting QoE and develop their mapping to scales like Mean Opinion Score for 2D content. Today, the digital video world is on the eve of 3D imaging which is far more complex and sophisticated not only because of the involved technology but also due to the multi–factor nature of the overall 3D experience. This paper discusses the current state of the research on the emerging problem of the user perceived quality of 3D content.

Keywords: Quality of Experience, QoE, 3D Video, subjective tests, quality metrics.

1 Introduction

Nowadays we are experiencing a revolution in the production and delivery of multimedia — the common introduction of the 3D content to cinemas and home television. In the age of strong competition when multiple applications and equipment deliver similar functionality, the key to success is to provide users with the highest possible experience.

The first approach towards assessment of the quality of multimedia applications was based on the Quality of Service (QoS) parameters. However, in recent years it has been realised that the quality of experience depends much on other measurable parameters which arise during acquisition and compression of multimedia content. What is more it has been emphasised that the whole application delivery chain can impact the QoE (Quality of Experience), therefore parameters of the screening environment have to be taken into account as well.

* This publication is an output from a research project "Future Internet Engineering" POIG.01.01.02-00-045/09, part of the "Innovative Economy 2007-2013" programme co–funded by the European Union.

F. Alvarez and C. Costa (Eds.): UCMEDIA 2010, LNICST 60, pp. 69–75, 2012.

The quality assessment approach driven by all the factors influencing what users get and how they perceive imaging content has contributed to countless research problems. These problems encompass objective (numerical) quality metrics, subjective tests (MOS - Mean Opinion Score), a dilemma of full-reference (FR) and no-reference (NR) measurements, correlation and mapping between objective metrics and MOS, statistical tools specific for test data analysis, and even testing credibility and homo/heterogeneity of an end user pool. All that efforts have been raised to a ITU-T recommendation level.

The 3D content QoE research inherits all research problems which had to be previously solved for 2D QoE measurements. Moreover, new 3D-specific factors have to be taken into account, such as depth perception, naturalness and comfort of viewing. All these makes the researchers return to the drawing boards and start development of 3D QoE measurement methodology from scratch.

The rest of the paper is structured as follows. Section 2 presents the current state of the art of the QoE measurements of 3D content. Emerging research directions are described in section 3. The paper is summarised in section 4.

2   Quality of Experience

Any service provided to a customer is evaluated by him/her. Such judgement decides if a customer uses the service ever again. As QoS parameters are not enough to predict a customer experience special metrics and analysis are provided to predict QoE. In order to predict QoE value we have to measure a customer's (called further subject) subjective judgement. The most commonly used way to do so are subjective tests where a group of subjects judges the provided service quality. The VQEG group tests showed that with this methodology a high accuracy can be obtained [1].

The history of creating such precise specification shows that many different test have to be run in order to specify which viewing conditions have strong impact on the observed quality.

In order to properly measure QoE for 3D displays a similar work has to be done. Nevertheless, in 3D content there are more variables which have to be considered. Although all those problems are important, the most significant one which has to be solved is creating methodologies making it possible to compare different displays. Now the differences between different technologies are so significant that only custom metrics (i.e. metrics build for a specific display) can be proposed.

2.1   State of the Art of the 2D QoE Measurement Methods

Image and 2D video quality was extensively analysed over last few decades. The dawn of the quality assessment was dominated by simple statistics–based metrics (e.g. MSE or PSNR) utilised in performance evaluation of image and video compression schemes. Low correlation with the user experience (recent discussion is presented by Wang and Bovik in [2]) enforced necessity of more sophisticated approaches. Several full reference metrics (e.g. SSIM and VQM) utilising the human visual system properties were developed and successfully verified upon subjective results. Certain limitation of full reference approach (i.e. availability of the reference) brought to the market reduced and no reference metrics, capable of the absolute quality assessment. No reference metrics aim at evaluation of a certain artifacts, like noise, blur or blockiness, known prior to the metric design.

The majority of the existing metrics are devoted to the source quality and compression artifacts. Another important aspect of the video delivery chain is addressed by so called quality of delivery approach, trying to assess the perceived quality based on quality of service parameters. Another approach is the bit stream analysis which is currently being investigated by the Joint Effort Group within the Video Quality Experts Group [1].

2.2   Challenges of 3D Imaging

Three dimensional imaging systems try to imitate the human visual system. That is why there are many new challenges in field of perceived quality of experience assessment with respect to those involved when 2D content is analysed. In order to obtain depth perception sensation, a scene is captured from slightly different positions by stereo cameras (either real or virtual) which actually take over the role of the eyes.

There are four main 3D content visualisation criteria that are analysed in literature: image quality, naturalness, viewing experience and depth perception. In terms of the depth preception criterion six important aspects must be considered: binocular disparity and stereopsis[3], accommodation and vergence[4], asymmetrical binocular combination and individual differences (stereoblindness, strabismus, interpupillary distance, age, display duration etc.). Human visual system to construct a perception of depth utilises monoculary available information (or cues) such as accommodation, occlusion, linear and aerial perspective, relative density, and motion parallax. The effectiveness of monocular cues can be easily proven by closing one eye and noticing a considerable appreciation of depth, the binocular cues, stereopsis and vergence, require both eyes to work together [5]. What is more, the accuracy of depth perception is strictly depending on *consistency* of specified cues.

2.3   3D Content Creation, Delivery and Presentation

Nowadays a lot of effort is being made to produce binocular stereopsis by means of delivering different images to each eye separately. Aided stereoscopic display is one of such methods. In general, separation of L and R views is achieved using specialised glasses. The simplest separation is done by colour filtration. This old method is called anaglyph. Unfortunately, the method produces strong color artifacts and is hardly acceptable by the audience. More advanced method is used in Dolby3D systems. It utilises complex multiband filters in order to separate video stream for each eye. This method produces better visual quality but requires expensive glasses and substantially decreases brightness. Light polarisation is another very popular method used in the IMAX cinemas, which is able to divide video streams by means of either linear or circular polarisation of the light. This method, applied in 3D IMAX cinema, requires dedicated projectors as well as non-depolarising screens. The last glasses–based solution employs shutters build from liquid–crystal. It is believed to be the most advanced separation technology. It requires double refresh rate capable screen, usually 120Hz, and is used in modern 3D LCD (Liquid Crystal Display) and Plasma displays as well as in some cinema systems.

Binocular head mounted displays (HMD) is another solution for 3D vision creation. It utilises active LCD or OLED (Organic Light Emitting Diode) displays mounted in front of each eye separately and thus, provides the most accurate channel separation. Since image depends on the head position, it has to be generated on–line. That is why HMD is practically limited to the virtual generated environment such as 3D games, simulations and medical applications.

Autostereoscopic displays are very attractive for the audience as glasses are not required for the 3D effect. This technology makes use of spatial multiplexing of left and right image by means of parallax barrier or microlens solution. Biggest shortcoming of spatial multiplexing is so called "sweet spot". Depending on the relative eye and screen position 3D image appears as depth-correct or incorrect (inverse depth). What is more, sweet spots tend to be narrow and thus, very confusing.

All the methods presented above may suffer from 3D distortions such as: optical cross talk, lack of motion parallax, wrong perspective, unbalanced colour, brightness reduction, insufficient refresh rate, etc. Some of them could be compensated by means of digital signal processing.

Since the most popular method of 3D content creation rely on delivery of two correlated video streams, it is easy to deal with compression by extensions of well known standards. For example, Multiview Video Coding (MVC) is an extension of H.264/AVC [6]. What is more, correlation between streams makes it possible to achieve better compression ratio than for two separate streams. It is also possible to encode 3D image as 2D image plus depth [7]. Such an approach requires reconstruction of 3D positional information using signal processing methods.

3D video content creation is usually done by simultaneous recording from multiple view points. Camera could be either real or virtual. 3D camera could mimic human visual system by means of two lenses separated by the distance of human's eyes (64 mm) or the 3D sensation could be achieved by processing of multiple video streams [8]. It is also possible to add depth to the 2D movies by digital video processing [9].

2.4   QoE of 3D Video

The quality assessment for 3D video applications is a much more complicated task than for 2D. The reason for this is that the overall 3D experience can be described as a combination of both 2D image quality and factors introduced by the 3rd dimension (as discussed in section 2.2). The only aspect covered up to date by the plethora of 2D quality metrics is the image quality. All other aspects of 3D quality are currently new research directions.

The relationship between three 2D video objective metrics (PSNR, SSIM and VQM) and the subjective results are analysed for 3D video content affected with network losses in [10]. Two video standards are considered, namely stereo (left and right images) and colour plus depth. Stereo sequences were screened using PC monitors with shutter glasses, while colour and depth were screened using autostereoscopic displays. Obtained results suggest strong correlation of the objective metrics with the subjective image quality and depth perception.

In [11] the authors present how the quality of 3D video encoded using H.264 as color plus depth is affected by the different bit budgets allocated for color and depth. The 3D quality was estimated using two quality metrics dedicated for 2D video material, namely PSNR and VSSIM (Video SSIM). Obtained results suggests that in order to optimize the overall 3D quality depth should be encoded with 15% - 20% of the available bit rate. The result obtained using objective metrics were verified in small subjective experiment.

A joint source channel coding scheme (JSCC) for color and depth 3D video was proposed in [12]. The proposed coding schema aims at optimization of the overall 3D experience for transmission over loss prone WiMAX network. The results show that the overall 3D experience is dominated by the color component. In consequence, higher bit rate and stronger protection should be allocated for this component. The overall image quality, the depth perception and the overall 3D experience were rated in the subjective experiment. It was also shown that the overall 3D experience can be fairly close approximated by a single 3D perceptual attribute or even by 2D objective quality metric.

In [13] the authors present an effect of the depth compression on the 3D perception, for sequences in colour plus depth standard. For the purpose of the experiment the depth component was compressed using H.264 and different bit rates. Prepared test set was screened using autostereoscopic displays. Subjective results show than the depth component may be significantly compressed while sustaining high 3D quality.

The above consideration contains a clear message that the overall quality metric suited for 3D does not exist. Current efforts tend to make use of existing 2D metrics even without any adaptation. The conclusion is simple — a design of the quality metric dedicated for 3D video content is a big challenge.

3 Emerging Trends

The 3D QoE is a fairly new research area. There are several research projects and organisations which put a lot of effort into development of the 3D quality metrics. This section provides a brief overview of the 3D QoE research initiatives.

3.1 VQEG

The VQEG (Video Quality Experts Group) [1] has recently started to point its attention to 3DTV video quality metrics and models. This activity is related to the ITU-R Question 128/6.

The group at first will try to investigate ways of measuring 3D quality, which will be followed be the development of standard metrics and models. These tasks differ significantly from previous VQEG efforts towards 2D models. It is not straightforward to transfer 2D expertise into the 3D area. For example, apart from classical image quality aspects, metrics for depth map quality, presentation room quality or viewing comfort quality (how long the user can watch 3D) have to be developed. Furthermore, some of the problems that have been already solved for 2D video technology, like blurriness, strike back in the 3D technology (such as crosstalk leading to ghosting images). The currently available quality metrics for stereoscopic images are not enough as they have been based on 2D ground-truth. Nevertheless, current creation of 3D video quality metrics is hampered by a lack of high quality and realistic reference content. In order to gather a reference test-set of 3D videos, a CDVL (The Consumer Digital Video Library) [14] library is currently being extended to accept and provide 3D content as well.

The currently investigated problems that may affect the perceived 3D video quality, include also screen luminance (being not equal to perceived luminance), monitor resolutions problems, viewing distances, depth rendering, depth of focus and naturalness. Other considered aspects take account of analysis of planes of stereoscopic voxels (3D pixels), depth resolution, depth rendering ability, number of planes within the focus range, comfortable viewing zone, angular depth plane interval, and field of view. More information about topics related to 3D quality metrics, being under investigation of VQEG member can be found in [15]. Complementary activities in this area have been initiated in the ICDM (International Committee for Display Metrology) group as well [16].

3.2 "Future Internet Engineering"

In January 2010 a Polish national project "Future Internet Engineering" was inaugurated with a total budget of approx. 10M EUR. The overall goal of the project is to develop and test the infrastructure and services for the future generation Internet. One of tasks of the project is to develop a measurement methodology for the 3D video and services. The research will cover not only the quality of 3D video but also the user perceived quality of 3D environments, such as virtual museums and the QoE of the user interfaces implemented in the 3D environments.

4 Summary

The presented position paper reminds the readership Quality of Experience issues that strongly affect design, development, and deployment of imaging services. As 2D imaging applications in most cases do involve end user perception little is known how QoE point of view will impact 3D imaging applications. The paper points to specific 3D challenges across a whole delivery chain and summarises some ongoing research projects.

References

1. VQEG, The Video Quality Experts Group, http://www.vqeg.org/
2. Wang, Z., Bovik, A.C.: Mean squared error: love it or leave it? - a new look at signal fidelity measures. IEEE Signal Processing Magazine 26(1), 98–117 (2009)
3. Woo, G., Sillanpaa, V.: Absolute stereoscopic threshold as measured by crossed and uncrossed disparities. American Journal of Optometry and Physiological Optics (56), 350–355 (1979)
4. Lambooij, M.T.M., Ijsselsteijn, W.A., Heynderickx, I.: Visual comfort of binocular and 3d displays. In: Visual Discomfort in Stereoscopic Displays: a Review, in Stereoscopic Displays and Virtual Reality Systems XIV. Proceedings of SPIE, vol. 6490, pp. 1–13 (January 2007)
5. Wijnand, A.I., Seuntins, P.J.H., Meesters, L.M.J.: Human factors of 3d displays. In: 3D Videocommunication - Algorithms, Concepts and Real-Time Systems in Human Centred Communication, pp. 219–233. John Wiley and Sons Ltd. (2005)
6. Merkle, P., Smolic, A., Muller, K., Wiegand, T.: Efficient prediction structures for multiview video coding. IEEE Transactions on Circuits and Systems for Video Technology 17(11), 1461–1473 (2007)
7. Smolic, A., Mueller, K., Merkle, P., Kauff, P., Wiegand, T.: An overview of available and emerging 3d video formats and depth enhanced stereo as efficient generic solution. In: Picture Coding Symposium, PCS 2009, pp. 1–4 (May 2009)
8. Hartley, R.I., Zisserman, A.: Multiple View Geometry in Computer Vision, 2nd edn. Cambridge University Press (2004) ISBN: 0521540518
9. Würmlin, S., Lamboray, E., Staadt, O.G., Gross, M.H.: 3d video recorder. In: PG 2002: Proceedings of the 10th Pacific Conference on Computer Graphics and Applications, p. 325. IEEE Computer Society, Washington, DC (2002)
10. Yasakethu, S.L.P., Hewage, C., Fernando, W., Kondoz, A.: Quality analysis for 3d video using 2d video quality models. IEEE Transactions on Consumer Electronics 54(4), 1969–1976 (2008)
11. Tikanmaki, A., Gotchev, A., Smolic, A., Miller, K.: Quality assessment of 3d video in rate allocation experiments. In: IEEE International Symposium on Consumer Electronics, ISCE 2008, April 14-16, pp. 1–4 (2008)
12. Yasakethu, S.L.P., Fernando, W.A.C., Kamolrat, B., Kondoz, A.: Analyzing perceptual attributes of 3d video. IEEE Transactions on Consumer Electronics 55(2), 864–872 (2009)
13. Leon, G., Kalva, H., Furht, B.: 3d video quality evaluation with depth quality variations. In: 3DTV Conference: The True Vision - Capture, Transmission and Display of 3D Video, May 28-30, pp. 301–304 (2008)
14. CDVL, The Consumer Digital Video Library, http://www.cdvl.org/
15. Chen, W., Fournier, J., Barkowsky, M., Callet, P.L.: New Requirements of Subjective Video Quality Assessment Methodologies for 3DTV. In: Fifth International Workshop on Video Processing and Quality Metrics for Consumer Electronics, Scottsdale, Arizona, U.S.A. (January 2010), http://www.vpqm.org/
16. ICDM, International Committee for Display Metrology, http://icdm-sid.org/

Depth Based Perceptual Quality Assessment
for Synthesised Camera Viewpoints

Erhan Ekmekcioglu, Stewart Worrall, Demuni De Silva,
Anil Fernando, and Ahmet M. Kondoz

I-Lab Multimedia Communications Research Group
University of Surrey
Guildford GU2 7XH, Surrey, United Kingdom

Abstract. This paper considers the visual quality assessment for view synthesis in the context of 3D video delivery chain. It is targeted to perceptually quantify the reconstruction quality of synthesised camera viewpoints. It is needed for developing better QoE models related to 3D-TV, as well as for a better representation of the effect of depth maps on views synthesis quality. In this paper, existing 2D video quality assessment methods, like PSNR and SSIM, are extended to assess the perceived quality of synthesised viewpoints based on the depth range. The performance of the extended assessment techniques is measured by correlating multiple sample video assessment scores to that of the Video Quality Metric (VQM) scores, which are a robust reflector of real subjective opinions.

Keywords: 3DTV, Free-viewpoint Video, Video Quality Assessment, Depth Map, Multi-view Video.

1 Introduction

The quality assessment of video has been a challenging research task. The subjective assessment is very time consuming, costly and cannot definitely be conducted in real time. PSNR cannot accurately model the perceptual quality, since the human perception of image/video distortions and human visual system properties are not taken into account [1]. Video Quality Metric (VQM) [2] measures the perceptual attributes of various video impairments and combines them into a single metric. Despite its complexity, VQM has high correlation with subjective video quality assessment.

For stereoscopic video, a number of quality assessment methodologies are available, although there is not yet a universal standard. PSNR does not give information about depth perception. The reason is that the attributes associated with 2D video cannot be directly used in measuring the real naturalness, depth perception and the overall image quality of 3D video. In [3], it is found that the output from the VQM metric can be mapped so that it correlates strongly with both the overall viewer perception of image quality and depth perception.

F. Alvarez and C. Costa (Eds.): UCMEDIA 2010, LNICST 60, pp. 76–83, 2012.

The quality assessment of arbitrary camera viewpoint synthesis via a pair of cameras is also an open research issue. Especially, the recent advancements in 3D-TV delivery systems necessitate the correct analysis of synthesised viewpoints that drive next generation multi-view displays. One of them is the 3D HD multimedia delivery chain envisaged in the recent EU ICT FP7 project called DIOMEDES that aims at content aware 3D delivery. In the same context, by incorporating the effect of depth maps on the perceived visual quality, better depth extraction and compression algorithms can be generated. In [4] authors have analysed the effect of depth map compression on the geometric distortions generated in the 3D space and accordingly on synthesised camera viewpoints. In [5], authors have implemented a mode decision algorithm for depth map compression in 3D-TV systems based on the effect on view synthesis without saliency adaptation. The work presented in this paper proposes a depth range and depth consistency based adaptation for the view synthesis quality assessment that will improve both the multi-view depth estimation and compression within DIOMEDES.

The 3D Video (3DV) Ad Hoc group formed under MPEG utilises a modified version of PSNR to evaluate the quality of view synthesis, which is called PSPNR (Peak Signal to Perceptual Noise Ratio) [6]. The authors in [6] introduce a Just Noticeable Difference (JND) model into pixel categorization, which is based on some human visual system traits. However, this technique doesn't take into consideration any kind of adaptation to the scene depth.

Based on the knowledge that low depth areas are more vulnerable to rendering distortions than high depth areas, this paper proposes an unequal weighting based quality evaluation approach to be applied on most commonly used 2D video quality assessment tools: PSNR and SSIM. The weighting is based on the scene depth information. The proposed framework also takes into consideration the scene motion activity in time and adapts a factor in the final score, that is related to temporal consistency of non-moving background objects during view synthesis.

Section 2 presents the proposed framework. Section 3 gives the details of the experiments and discusses the results. Section 4 gives the subjective evaluation results to justify the results in section 3. Finally, section 4 concludes the paper.

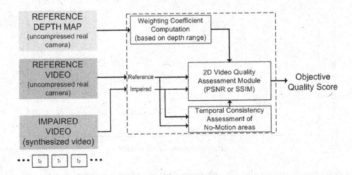

Fig. 1. Block diagram illustration of the proposed view synthesis quality assessment framework

2   Proposed Virtual Viewpoint Quality Assessment Framework

The proposed framework includes depth range and scene motion activity adaptive partitioning of error map. Accordingly, the final score of view synthesis quality per video frame is computed as the weighted average of the corresponding error map, where the weighting is performed via the mentioned adaptation. Figure 1 shows the illustrative block diagram of the overall process. The reference video signal is a captured video and the reference uncompressed depth map represents the original scene depth information from the corresponding viewpoint (where the synthesis takes place). The impaired video signal is the synthesised camera viewpoint. According to the weighting coefficient calculation process during quality assessment, some video frame regions, which are far away from the capturing camera, are given less importance when incorporating them in the overall visual quality score and some frame sections are given zero importance which makes them get excluded during error signal computation.

The next two sub-sections describe the weighting coefficient computation based on scene depth information, temporal consistency assessment in no-motion video frame sections.

2.1   Weighting Computation Based on Depth Range

In measuring the objective quality of a video frame, all pixels or blocks are assigned the same weight in contributing to the final frame quality. In a synthesised video frame, it is more likely to observe rendering related distortions in the vicinity of front objects. Assuming that human visual perception is more affected by the distortions happening on the front part of the scene it is planned to give more weight to such frame regions in calculating the 'perceived' frame distortion.

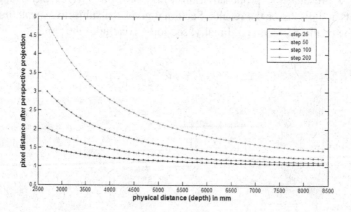

Fig. 2. Pixel distance between the neighbouring pixels after perspective projection, where the step sizes in mm represent the depth difference between the neighbouring pixels

The weighting coefficients assigned to individual video frame pixels vary between 0 and 1. In the proposed approach, the weighting coefficient function is selected as a piecewise linear function, where the weighting coefficient becomes 0 when the local scene depth is above a certain upper threshold (Z_f) and becomes 1 when the local scene depth is under a certain lower threshold (Z_n). In the depth zone, which lies between the corresponding lower and upper thresholds, the weighting coefficients change linearly, inversely proportional to the local scene depth range. Equation 1 depicts this.

$$WC(x,y)=\begin{cases} 0, & Z(x,y)>Z_f \\ \dfrac{(Z(x,y)-Z_f)}{(Z_n-Z_f)}, & Z_n \leq Z(x,y) \leq Z_f \\ 1, & Z(x,y)<Z_n \end{cases} \tag{1}$$

$WC(x,y)$ stands for the weighting coefficient at the corresponding pixel position (x,y) in the video frame. Similarly, $Z(x,y)$ refers to the physical distance (depth) of the corresponding pixel position (x,y). Z_n and Z_f are the lower and the upper threshold depth values, which represent the sensitivity levels of the textural connectivity of corresponding video frame regions to break-downs during view synthesis. Considering two neighbour pixels in the source viewpoint, (x,y) and $(x-1,y)$, a certain amount of depth difference, which is not expected to break the connectivity between them after warping to another viewpoint may cause so, if the depth levels of them are sufficiently low. Considering the pinhole camera model and using the computation of coordinate transforms, the horizontal pixel distance Δd between these two neighbour pixels after warping to the coordinates of the target viewpoint (C') is

$$\Delta d = 1 + a \cdot \frac{Z(x-1,y)-Z(x,y)}{Z(x-1,y)\cdot Z(x,y)} \tag{2}$$

where a is a constant derived from the rotational, translational and affine parameters of the source and target viewpoints. The graph shown in Figure 2 depicts the computed Δd value according to the pixel's depth values. The physical distance axis corresponds to $Z(x,y)$. Several depth differences between neighbour pixels are considered (from 25 mm to 200 mm apart). Z_f is defined as the depth value $min(Z(x,y), Z(x-1,y))$ such that $\Delta d = 1$. Pixels with a depth value greater than Z_f are not vulnerable to separation and visual distortion after warping, for a pre-determined step depth difference. Similarly, Z_n is defined as the depth value $min(Z(x,y), Z(x-1,y))$ such that $\Delta d = 2$. Pixels with a lower depth than Z_n, are separated by more than 1 pixels after perspective projection and therefore, the corresponding frame regions are subject to visual distortions. Hence, such frame sections are given most significance by assigning them the highest coefficient, when computing the overall perceptual frame distortion.

2.2 Temporal Consistency Assessment in Motionless Frame Regions

The proposed virtual viewpoint quality assessment framework also takes into account the temporal consistency among successive synthesised frames. This functionality is achieved by considering the motion activity in both the synthesised video and the original video. Basically, motionless frame regions might have suspiciously high motion activity in the synthesised video, causing a flickering effect.

First, the frame absolute difference D_o is computed between the current time colour texture frame and the previous time colour texture frame of the original camera (O), such as

$$D_o = |O(t) - O(t-1)| \qquad (3)$$

Second, the frame absolute difference D_s is also computed between the current time colour texture frame and the previous time colour texture frame of the synthesised camera (S), such as

$$D_s = |S(t) - S(t-1)| \qquad (4)$$

At pixel locations (x,y), if $D_o(x,y) < m$, where m represents a motion activity threshold, and $D_s(x,y) > m$, then the corresponding pixel locations are flagged as temporally suspicious pixels with a risk of flickering. Hence, a coefficient of '1' is given to such pixels, where a '0' coefficient is given to all remaining pixels, during the frame temporal difference calculation. The frame temporal difference metric is selected either as PSNR or SSIM, where the reference video frame is the previous time instant frame of the synthesised video source and the impaired video frame is the current time instant frame of the synthesised video source. The calculated total temporal frame synthesis error corresponds to the total amount of flickering activity which is not present in the original camera source.

Once the two sets of weighting coefficients are computed, they are multiplied with the calculated error frame. Error frame indicates the calculated MSE map if PSNR is utilised or the calculated structural similarity index map if SSIM is utilised. The corresponding final objective score *Final* is computed as

$$Final(n) = c_1 \cdot Final_s(n) + c_2 Final_t(n) \qquad (5)$$

where n is the frame index, and subscripts s and t correspond to the final scores considering the depth range adaptation and the temporal consistency check, respectively. c_1 and c_2 are the coefficients of individual metrics that contribute to the overall perceived distortion. In this case, this relationship is assumed to be additive and the contributions from each is considered to be equal, i.e. $c_1 = c_2 = 0.5$.

3   Experimental Results

To evaluate the performance of the proposed framework, a number of camera viewpoints are synthesised using colour texture videos and depth maps, with various kinds of artefacts added to them. Two different multi-viewpoint video sequences (*Akko&Kayo* and *Newspapers*) are used in the experiments. For each test video sequence, two target camera viewpoints (camera #1 from cameras #0 and #2, camera #2 from cameras #1 and #3) are used for view synthesis.

To distort colour texture video sequences, two different quantisation step sizes are used. For distorting the depth map sequences, four different operations are utilised, one deployed each time. One source of distortion is the quantisation distortion. The second source of distortion is added via passing the depth map videos through a low pass filter (by down-sampling and up-sampling with a ratio of ½ and 2, respectively). In this way, the high frequency components in the depth map videos are eliminated. The third source of artificial distortion is added by shifting the object borders. In the experiments, the object borders in the depth map videos are shifted to left and right separately, by 5 pixels. The final source of distortion is introduced to the depth map videos by adding artificial local spot errors in certain regions to create temporal inconsistency in the synthesised videos. All combinations of distorted colour texture and depth map video sequences are used for synthesising the test videos. In total, 64 different synthesised videos are used for quality assessment experiments.

The performances of six different objective quality metrics are computed, taking the VQM scores as the reference, i.e. as mean subjective opinions. It is chosen as such, because VQM [2] has a high correlation with the subjective assessment scores despite its computational complexity.

Table 1 shows the correlation coefficient results of the mentioned objective quality assessment methods.

When the proposed framework is applied on the conventional PSNR metric, an increase by 0.012 and 0.088 in CC is obtained for *Akko&Kayo* and *Newspapers* sequences, respectively. In the case of SSIM metric, these numbers are 0.225 and 0.099, respectively. The improvements in the correlation coefficients are significant.

According to the results in Table 1, Spatial PSPNR and Temporal PSPNR metrics that are extended from the PSNR metric, show a better performance than the conventional PSNR metric in terms of assessing the perceptual video quality.

Table 1. Correlation coefficient scores of the evaluated objective metrics

Objective Metrics	Akko & Kayo	Newspapers
PSNR	CC = 0.960	CC = 0.884
PSNR with the proposed method	CC = 0.972	CC = 0.972
SSIM	CC = 0.505	CC = 0.408
SSIM with the proposed method	CC = 0.730	CC = 0.507
Spatial PSPNR	CC = 0.940	CC = 0.534
Temporal PSPNR	CC = 0.979	CC = 0.936

However, this improvement is not very significant. Excluding the Temporal PSPNR and comparing PSNR and Spatial PSPNR to each other, it is observed that the improvement in CC is in the range of 0.018 to 0.052.

Table 2. Subjective rankings for Akko & Kayo

AKKO&KAYO	Video 1	Video 2	Video 3	Video 4	Video 5	Video 6	Video 7	Video 8
Subjective Score	86.88855	84.08545	79.881	71.5772	70.57355	64.04767	43.84615	40.56818
Rank-order	1	2	3	4	5	6	7	8
PSNR	34.1840	34.1380	33.4930	32.0710	32.0350	31.7000	29.1270	29.2590
Rank order	1	2	3	4	5	6	8	7
PSNR with the proposed method	34.9230	34.9190	34.4620	33.4250	33.4050	33.1970	31.4520	31.4370
Rank order	1	2	3	4	5	6	7	8
T_PSPNR	48.4138	50.3212	48.7964	48.8010	48.4090	47.6594	39.1667	38.7101
Rank order	4	1	3	2	5	6	7	8
S_PSPNR	38.7588	38.6813	38.1170	36.2660	36.3585	35.8966	31.3540	31.2357
Rank order	1	2	3	5	4	6	7	8
VQM	0.021855	0.026174	0.09475	0.13477	0.14827	0.22379	0.76406	0.93805
Rank order	1	2	3	4	5	6	7	8

Table 3. Subjective rankings for Newspapers

NEWSPAPERS	Video 2	Video 4	Video 1	Video 6	Video 3	Video 5	Video 7	Video 8
Subjective Score	84.64283	78.7608	78.46629	76.147	71.76583	60.227	42.91515	40
Rank order	1	2	3	4	5	6	7	8
PSNR	29.462	29.025	29.562	29.097	29.105	29.482	26.814	25.457
Rank order	3	6	1	5	4	2	7	8
PSNR with the proposed method	34.936	34.817	34.929	34.757	34.771	34.575	32.504	31.702
Rank order	1	3	2	4	5	6	7	8
T_PSPNR	49.7091	49.5248	47.1042	47.2766	47.0979	42.7410	39.8070	41.8790
Rank order	1	2	4	3	5	6	8	7
S_PSPNR	33.3700	32.8460	33.5276	32.9877	32.9741	33.3267	28.4411	26.5890
Rank order	2	6	1	4	5	3	7	8
VQM	0.010308	0.009946	0.030746	0.035713	0.037317	0.045392	0.42216	1
Rank order	1	2	3	4	5	6	7	8

4   Subjective Test Results

To further justify the performance of the proposed framework applied on the conventional video quality evaluation methods, subjective tests are conducted using a subset of the synthesised test videos. 15 non-expert subjects are asked to assess the visual quality of different synthesised videos (from 1 to100) in random order, taking the original camera view as reference. For each test, the standard deviation of the subject's opinion is calculated and accordingly, the outliers are eliminated. Table 2 and Table 3 show the average subjective scores as well as the scores of PSNR, PSNR with the proposed framework, S_PSPNR and T_PSPNR for Akko&Kayo and Newspapers sequences, respectively. The quality ranking order of each synthesised video for the corresponding objective assessment metrics as well as subjective scores, are provided on each table. The results verify the assumption that VQM can be used as a robust reflector of the subjective scores. According to the results, the quality ranking according to the metric on which the proposed framework is applied, has a better correlation with the quality ranking according to the subject opinion than the quality ranking according to S_PSPNR.

5   Conclusion

This paper addressed the issue of evaluating the perceptual quality of the synthesised videos to be considered within the 3D-TV delivery systems. A new full-reference perceptual quality assessment framework is designed and tested using some state-of-the-art video quality assessment metrics, like PSNR and SSIM. The proposed framework assigns more importance to regions of a synthesised frame that are relatively more open to synthesis related distortions. This is achieved by exploiting the depth map at the target camera position. Another feature of the proposed framework is that temporal consistency is tracked within the synthesised videos. Accordingly, better performance is achieved in reflecting real subject opinions, with respect to PSNR, SSIM and PSPNR. The presented quality assessment idea can be incorporated with multi-view depth estimation and coding systems for better 3D scene reconstruction quality in high quality entertainment multimedia delivery.

Acknowledgement. This work has been supported by the DIOMEDES (*Distribution of Multi-View Entertainment Using Content Aware Delivery Systems*) project, funded under the European Commission ICT 7th Framework Programme (www.diomedes-project.eu).

References

[1] Girod, B.: What's wrong with Mean-Squared Error. In: Watson, A.B. (ed.) Digital Images and Human Vision, ch. 15, pp. 207–220. The MIT Press (1993)

[2] Pinson, M.H., Wolf, S.: A new standardized method for objectively measuring video quality. IEEE Transactions on Broadcasting 50(3), 312–322 (2004)

[3] Hewage, C.T.E.R., Worrall, S., Dogan, S., Kondoz, A.M.: Quality Evaluation of Colour plus Depth Map Based Stereoscopic Video. IEEE Journal of Selected Topics in Signal Processing 3(2), 304–318 (2009)

[4] Merkle, P., Morvan, Y., Smolic, A., Farin, D., Mueller, K., de With, P.H.N., Wiegand, T.: The Effects of Multiview Depth Video Compression on Multiview Rendering. Signal Processing: Image Communication 24, 73–88 (2009)

[5] De Silva, D., Fernando, W.A.C., Kodikara Arachchi, H.: A New Mode Selection Technique for Coding Depth Maps of 3D Video. In: IEEE International Conference on Acoustics, Speech and Signal Processing (ICASSP 2010), Dallas (March 2010)

[6] Zhao, Y., et al.: Perceptual measurement for evaluating quality of view synthesis. In: MPEG Doc. M16407, Maui, USA (April 2009)

GeoMedia – A Framework for Producing Interactive, Geo-Referenced Video Contents

Andrei Papliatseyeu[1], Givoanni Cortese[2], and Oscar Mayora-Ibarra[1]

[1] CREATE-NET, Via alla Cascata 56C, Trento Italy
[2] Interplay Software, Trento, Italy
{andrei.papliatseyeu,g.cortese}@ipsoft.it,
oscar.mayora@create-net.org

Abstract. This work-in-progress paper presents an approach for interactive geo-localized multimedia services. The GeoMedia platform will provide richer user experience within the context of city-level cultural or sport events. This will be achieved by means of media aggregation using geo-references and multi-view of pictures and videos aligned with the geospatial coordinate system. The composed imagery/video will be made available for the event participants via their mobile devices, such as smartphones. This will enable the users to reconstruct recent scenes and situations at certain locations of the medium-scale event, thus augmenting the participation experience.

Keywords: Geo-referenced content, location based services, context awareness.

1   Introduction

The advances of scientific knowledge in the fields of multimedia information management and augmented reality, and the increasing spread of enabling technologies (such as broadband connectivity and mobile handsets with advanced multimedia features) creates the adequate conditions for the development of new services for the web based on interactive video contents. In particular through images geo-registration techniques, it becomes possible to create interactive video geo-located, where the user can explore the space / scene depicted in the video, or change the observation point, or obtain information about a monument in the video by clicking on it [1]. This enables users to live a stronger experience of presence in the scene and the realism of it.

Mobile phones and smartphones are obviously ideal devices for capturing and utilizing multimedia content strongly related to the physical world [2, 3]. The application of interactive geo-located multimedia services has a large target market, and gathers different market sectors and applications (such as promoting tourism, cultural heritage, e-commerce, e-learning, asset management and public works) [4]. The growing competition in the tourism industry and the need for promotion and enhancement of local resources creates a continuous demand of innovation in the modalities for communication and marketing on the web. In the scope of activities

F. Alvarez and C. Costa (Eds.): UCMEDIA 2010, LNICST 60, pp. 84–90, 2012.

relevant to the promotion of tourism, an interesting scenario is that of sports and cultural events. Organizers of such events often require advanced tools for making information services or providing advanced collaboration tools benefiting the organization of participants and the spectators. To date, the state-of-the-art knowledge and current tools available for implementing interactive geo-localized multimedia services are very much at the research level, or still too expensive for widespread use. This paper presents an approach to make more immediate use of current knowledge and techniques for geo-localized applications in targeted contexts (such as massive sports or cultural events).

2   GeoMedia Scenario

The context which is taken as reference for the GeoMedia scenario is that of a massive event in a medium-size city (e.g. sport, cultural, touristic event). In this scenario, the organizers of the event intend to create services focused on provisioning multimedia content for the different participants and for spectators and tourists. An example of this could be the next Nordic Sky World Championship to be hosted in Trentino province of Italy. For this event it is planned that the main competitions will be on an extended area, partly or wholly equipped with network infrastructure such as Wi-Fi, or 3G. The organizers of the event will have an infrastructure capable of providing access to the web to visitors and other general users and an intranet with restricted access for specialized users (journalists, premium users). This reserved access network will provide special information and other added value services to participants of the event. One of such geo-localized services is the access to geo-referenced media. In this way, the special users will be able to reconstruct the recent events and situations that happen at certain locations of the sky track (e.g. pictures/videos of participants in that point) at different moments.

3   GeoMedia Framework

GeoMedia framework consists of a set of methods, algorithms and architectural approaches allowing organizers of city-level events to benefit the participants with the possibility of creating interactive video content using a new type of media aggregation including geo-references and multi-view. In this way, GeoMedia aims to communicate to the viewer a sense of involvement and engagement with the system and generally a richer sensory experience. The main feature of the contents produced with GeoMedia will be the possibility of being created from "imagery" being captured from photo / video cameras and sensors for positioning and orientation and recorded and aligned with a geospatial coordinate system. Thanks to this feature the presentation of content in GeoMedia will enable the multiple view of pictures considering the different geometry of the physical space represented in the video. GeoMedia enables the composition and production of imagery and interactive video, which are then made available to participants of the event via their smartphones. Even during the delivery / use of content, the system's ability to acquire and interpret the position in space of the user, and therefore optimize the presentation of content (Context-awareness) will be one of the main features of GeoMedia framework.

The following figure schematically represents the GeoMedia system (Figure 1). The main components of the system highlight the different functionalities enabled by the system such as the presentation of videos in 3D environment, geo-referenced registration of video/images, scene analysis, etc) and architectural approaches (e.g. localization methods, techniques for determination of the camera position, encoding of geospatial information into the video stream, etc.).

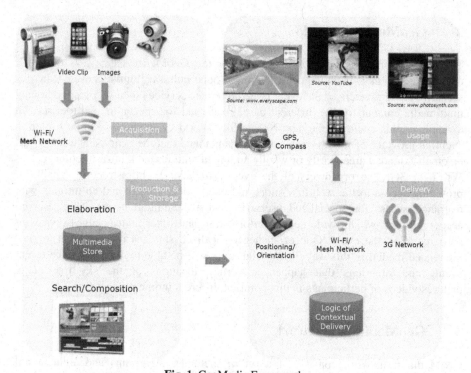

Fig. 1. GeoMedia Framework

The main components of GeoMedia framework include:

1. Acquisition Component
2. Pre-processing
3. Delivery
4. Presentation

<u>Acquisition Component:</u> In the acquisition phase, images and videos are acquired by consumer devices such as mobile phones, webcams, photo/video cameras, etc. These devices will be enriched when needed with other sensors for the acquisition of position and orientation information (GPS, compass, tilt sensors). The acquisition of

audiovisual content can occur either in the stage of organization of the event (for example, the creation of an interactive video that documents and allows to visualize the race route) and during the event itself (e.g. photo/video of the races). The multimedia information and location is transmitted to the content management system, using a network (e.g. mesh or Wi-Fi), or via removable storage devices.

Pre-processing: The pre-processing and analysis software processes the images and position data, extracting useful information for further processing. The geolocalized images are stored in a scalable repository equipped with advanced search functionality to find pictures on the basis of geospatial criteria. A set of software tools (Authoring framework) thus allows authorized users to access and edit the material of the CMS, and create presentations that will be published and made available to the end users. Some examples of authoring capabilities that will allow manipulation of multimedia and creation of interactive videos include: the creation of clips, composition, textual or graphical annotations (e.g. graffiti), creation of hyperlinks to other content media.

Delivery: The front-end towards the end user is represented by a delivery service that will be optimized for the transmission of interactive video to mobile terminals and the delivery of location-based information.

Presentation: The presentation at the end user side will be accessible through an intranet portal available from dedicated fixed terminals, interactive kiosks or mobile terminals. The information will be presented using video players enabled with graphics and control features for advanced interaction.

Finally, an appropriate network architecture consistent with the envisioned application scenarios will ultimately provide the required infrastructure for the proper functioning of services.

4   GeoMedia Positioning and Geo-Tagging System

The GeoMedia system distinguishes two types of users: stationary and mobile ones. Stationary users are provided with a web interface, which displays a world map and a number of marked locations on it. In GeoMedia, a location is defined by a pair of coordinates and a name (e.g., "Shopping mall"). Each location has a number of virtual stickers associated with it. A sticker contains a multimedia file, its description and priority level. Stationary users can modify and add new locations, as well as upload new stickers.

Mobile users are equipped with location-aware devices that have Internet connectivity. The device periodically updates the system with the user's current position, and receives a list of nearby locations and stickers attached to them. When a new high-priority sticker is detected nearby, it is automatically downloaded and presented to the user; low-priority stickers can be received manually by user's request. In order to avoid abuse, the user can configure criteria of automatic downloading. The activity inference and prediction module is responsible for building user movements profile and using it to predict future context of the user.

The architecture of the location tagging system is presented on Figure 2. Both stationary and mobile clients communicate with the system by HTTP via web front-end. The Map Builder module takes map images from an online service, e.g. Google Maps, and overlays it with location markers. When the user selects a location, a list of associated stickers is displayed. The user can then upload a new sticker, and it will be attached to the selected location. For the mobile user, the process is more straight-forward: given the coordinates, the system generates an XML file with a list of locations and associated stickers in some vicinity of the user; basing on this list the mobile client downloads and displays stickers. However, the mobile part of the system presents a number of challenges, such as localization accuracy, limited resources, slow connections, privacy concerns, etc.

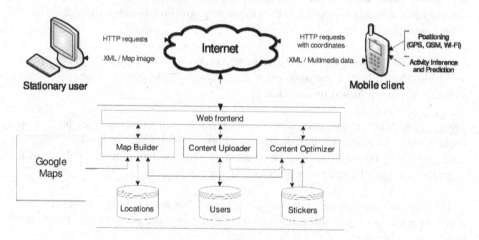

Fig. 2. Localization – Tagging System

To test the idea, we have implemented a single-user proto-type of the proposed localization-tagging system. Server part is running Apache Tomcat and Struts as web front-end; MySQL handles data management and storage. Stationary user's interface (see Figure 3) is based upon Google Maps API, using JavaScript for GUI management and AJAX for asynchronous communication with the server. Side panel displays the list of stickers associated with selected locations, and provides an interface for sticker upload. Only images are displayed directly in the browser, other types of content can be down- loaded and viewed by third-party applications.

The mobile client is implemented in Java 2 Micro Edition (J2ME) and runs on any MIDP2-enabled phone (Nokia E61i in our case). The current implementation uses Java Location API and GPS to obtain user position; later on we plan to adapt PlaceLab framework. User position is sent to the server via Wi-Fi, 3G or GPRS connection every 5 sec., which provides a reasonable trade-off between network load and system responsiveness. Privacy of the positioning data is secured by JSR-179 (Java Location API) regulations [5].

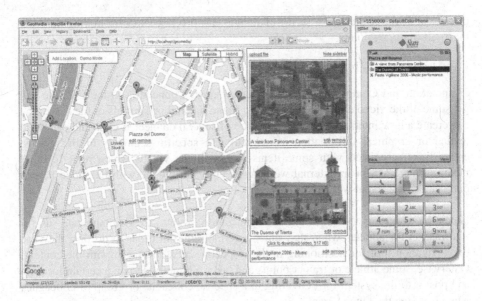

Fig. 3. Preliminary Web and Mobile Client Interfaces for Location-Tagging

5   GeoMedia Envisioned Services

The envisioned services of GeoMedia platform will be illustrated through some examples of possible applications inspired in the sports scenario mentioned above. The main services are divided according to the scenarios defined for both, the end users and the content creators.

Services for Content Consumers:

"Navigator" – Joe is a journalist who follows the event. Using a service offered by the Organizing Committee Joe can see the road races, represented in the form of an interactive video with navigation controls. The videos are annotations and "buttons" that allow him to view useful information, documents, pictures, videos, records of the competitors going through that location, etc. A variation of this service can consent to access information about nearby attractions, shops, restaurants, services and events in the area.

"What am I seeing" – Mary is watching the competitions close to the racetrack. She points an area in the racetrack with her phone video camera and the display gets a series of augmented descriptive information of the passage. On the image that is seeing are also offered a list of images / video clips relating to that passage (at precedent days, etc.).

"Media Alert" – Jan is an athlete in training. When approaching a specific area he is notified on his smartphone about the availability of video information that his trainer had previously registered on the site. By orienting the smartphone in different directions in the same site a series of images are proposed to him highlighting the most relevant viewpoints.

Services for Content Producers:

"Annotation and Composition" – Joe is a journalist. Connecting to the CMS he can get some of the video clips about the races. Using the authoring tools of the system he can create a new interactive video composed of several connected clips and can write textual or graphical information associated with specific segments of the videos, create links associated with some items shown in the videos which refer to other media in the CMS or in external web pages. Once hi is done with his video he can publish it to the Event webpage.

"Location Tagging" – The event organization wants to communicate useful information for athletes when they enter a certain area. In order to do this, they use the navigation tool for positioning in the respective area and tag it with the content. Otherwise, some athlete or trainer points and takes a photo/video on a certain location and post it to the system for delivering to a specific colleague or group of colleagues when reaching the tagged area.

6   Concluding Remarks

In this paper we presented a work in progress dedicated to building a framework for interactive geo-referenced multimedia provisioning. The main feature of the GeoMedia platform will be the possibility to create the content from "imagery" captured from photo/video cameras and align it with a geospatial coordinate system using positioning and orientation sensors. Thanks to this feature, the GeoMedia will be able to present the content from multiple views considering different geometry of the physical space represented in the video. The paper also described a number of location-based services which GeoMedia framework will enable.

References

1. Google Maps Street View. Online, http://books.google.com/help/maps/streetview
2. Ludford, P., Frankowski, D., Reily, K., Wilms, K., Terveen, L.: Because I Carry My Cell Phone Anyway: Functional Location-Based Reminder Applications. In: Proc. of CHI 2006, pp. 889–898. ACM Press (2006)
3. Marmasse, N., Schmandt, C.: Location-Aware Information Delivery with ComMotion. In: Thomas, P., Gellersen, H.-W. (eds.) HUC 2000. LNCS, vol. 1927, pp. 157–171. Springer, Heidelberg (2000)
4. Schiller, J.H., Voisard, A.: Location-based services (2004) ISBN: 978-1-55860-929-7
5. JSR 179: Location API for J2ME. Online, http://jcp.org/jsr/detail/179.jsp

A Classification Framework for Interactive Digital Artworks

Enrico Nardelli

Department of Mathematics
Univ. of Roma Tor Vergata, Roma, Italy
nardelli@mat.uniroma2.it

Abstract. We define Interactive Digital Artworks as Information Technology in-
tensive systems for which spectators are involved in the production of the artistic
output. We propose a novel framework for classification of interactive digital artworks built on the critical revision and refinement of previous work. Our approach
is based on the input-process-output view of Information Systems. The classification framework is validated by applying it to the classification of 54 interactive
digital artworks realized in Italy.

Keywords: Digital art, Interactive content production, Classification framework.

1 Introduction and Previous Work

By the term "Interactive Digital Artwork" (*IDA*, for short) we mean any artwork where
digital technology is an essential component and which is interactive (in the common
sense this word is used in IT). IDAs can be physical artworks placed in a public and
open space (usually called "installations") or virtual artworks enjoyed on a personal
device. Digital films/videos are usually not examples of IDA, nor is digital music, since
they both lack the contribution of the user to the content production. But when the
outcome of video animations or music pieces is modified according to user interaction
they are examples of "interactive digital art".

In [6] it is suggested that any computer artwork should be considered as an information systems and six research themes are proposed. More specifically, the following
three themes from [6] provide a context for our research:

- *Computer Art as an Information Systems*: each computer artwork can be abstracted
by the input-process-output reference scheme tipically used for Information Systems.
- *Computer Art and The Commercial Perspective*: this is about management and economic issues. How to establish the value of an IDA? What about copyright? Which are
the implications for IDA preservation for museum/gallery curators?
- *Computer Art as a Socio-Technical Systems*: Interactivity necessarily involves people
in the system and in [6] it is written: "We should ask whether our current understanding of participation in systems development applies equally to the creation of computer
artistic works".

Our research goal is to characterize and compare IDAs. To this aim we present a framework, or a scheme, that allows to arrange the various examples of IDAs in homogenous

F. Alvarez and C. Costa (Eds.): UCMEDIA 2010, LNICST 60, pp. 91–100, 2012.

classes or categories. Using this classification framework/scheme, in the following simply *classification*, it will therefore be easier to discussing and/or producing and/or buying interactive digital art.

In this respect our classification is similar to the ones used in the standard fine arts regarding, e.g., painting techniques (oil, watercolours, fresco, pastel, gouache, ...), materials (paper, wood, metal, stone, canvas, silk, ...), tools (brush, pencil, roller, chalk, ...), which makes it easier to discuss and to teach about artworks.

We based the structure of our classification framework on the review of relevant literature concerning this theme [8,4,3,9]. Then our classification is validated by considering (a subset of) the artworks discussed in the IDA literature and showing that they can be grouped according to our classification in a meaningful way.

The novelty of our proposal with respect to previous work is that it is explicitly based on the standard input-process-output view used for discussing Information Systems.

Previous work addressing our research goal was published in 1999 by Sommerer and Mignonneau [8], in 2002 by Hannington and Reed [4], in 2004 by Edmonds, Turner, and Candy [3], and in 2008 by Trifonova, Jaccheri, and Bergaust [9]. The main emphasis in all these classifications was on the user interaction. Hence all proposals were centered around the various kinds of interactions and did not consider the more general viewpoint of IDAs as Information Systems.

The older classification in the literature is the one discussed in [8], addressing "interactive artworks". Since it is not focusing on the use of information technology it is not able to characterize its specific aspects.

Then, the classification in [4] is covering "interaction in multimedia applications", hence it considers a larger and different set of works, since many multimedia applications have no artistic component.

Subsequently, the classification in [3] discusses "relationship between the artwork, artist, viewer and environment", hence it does not cover those internal aspects of the artwork that are related to the processing of input from the artwork audience, which is a very important aspect of an IDA.

Finally, the classification proposed in [9] addresses "interactive installation art": on the one side it hence considers a narrower set of works (just the installations and not the artworks experienced on personal devices, which are more and more important means for user interaction in the Future Internet), but on the other side it has been built by focusing just on interactivity as the main aspect of IDAs.

In the rest of the paper we first present our classification (Section 2), then compare it to previous ones (Section 3), and finally discuss its validation (Section 4).

2   The Classification Framework

An information system is conventionally seen as a system which **processes** a given **input** to produce a desired **output**. We consider an IDA in the same way, as a system which receives a certain input, called *content* in this context, and producing as a result the output intended by the IDA author (i.e., the artist). It is also helpful to consider the process producing the intended output as if it were a function in a mathematical sense, that is an abstract "device" which at each time instant transforms its inputs into its outputs according to its mathematical specification.

The dimensions of the classification are:

content provider: who produces the raw material processed by the IDA,
processing dynamics: which kind of variability has the processing itself,
processing contributors: which are the sources affecting the dynamics of processing.

For each dimension we now provide different values, that are the labels of our classification. We use the term *artist* to denote the person or team who has invented and realized the IDA, *audience* to denote the human beings actively and consciously providing any kind of input to the IDA, and *environment* to denote any passive or not-conscious entity present in the environment surrounding the IDA.

Regarding the **content provider** dimension, the source providing the content to the IDA can be either the *artist* or the *audience* or the *environment*. This dimension has therefore 3 possible values, or points, and an artwork can be labeled, with respect to this dimension, with one, two or all the values.

Regarding the **processing dynamics** dimension, the processing function of an artwork can be *static* with the passing of time, or it can be dynamic, that is changing as time passes. Note that the change considered here is the intrinsic change of the processing function, not a change in its input parameters. But the input parameters may determine, partly or wholly, such a change. In the case of a dynamic processing function, we consider three values, in mutual exclusion, to be used for a better characterization of the artwork:

- *predefined change*, where changes to the function follows the plan defined by the artist;
- *casual change*, where changes to the function derive by random choices, even in the case the set or the domain of the possible choices have been completely pre-defined by the artists;
- *evolutionary change*, where changes follow an unpredictable path defined by the evolution (in a biological sense) of the processing function itself.

The single value for the static case plus the three above values for the dynamic one give a total of 4 values (points) for this dimension. An artwork can be labeled with exactly one of these values.

Regarding the **processing contributors** dimension, the elements driving the content processing can be self-contained in the IDA (hence, what the *artist* has put directly inside the artwork affects the processing), or these elements can arrive at the IDA through the interaction with the context the IDA is placed within (that is, the processing function has additional input parameters causing modifications to how the content is processed). In the latter case, the providers of values changing the behavior of the processing function can be the *audience* or the *environment*. The dimension has therefore 3 values (points) and an artwork can receive one, two or all the labels.

Note that, in strictly mathematical terms, inputs to a functions are all equals, hence the distinction between "content provider" and "processing contributors" dimensions has no compelling mathematical reason. But from the artist viewpoint this differentiation is an important one, since it distinguishes between what she has directly inserted in the artwork and what arrives from the outside of the IDA, both in terms of the raw material and its processing function.

Also, an artwork labeled both under "content provider" exclusively with *artist* and under "processing contributors" exclusively with *artist* is **not** an IDA, since it has no elements of interaction at all. But as long as, in at least one of these two dimensions, the artwork is labeled with at least one more label, then it is an IDA.

The overall classification space is therefore made up by $3 \cdot 4 \cdot 3$ values or points. Each one of them can also be thought as a "labeled cell" containing all IDAs that can be classified with the labels corresponding to the point itself. Note that an IDA can be classified at the same time under more than one cell.

To give an example, let us consider an IDA taking pictures of its audience (say, one every five minutes) and displaying them while dynamically modifying them on the basis of data provided by the environment where the work is placed, so that each displayed picture is casually altered by one of the many processing filters defined by the artist, where the parameters guiding the filter are based on values read second by second in the environment. Then the classification label for such an IDA is: [**content provider**:*audience*, **processing dynamics**:*casual change*, **processing contributors**:*environment*].

A real IDA similar to this one is described in [7]: an installation which is inspired by Andy Warhol's statement that "In the future everybody will be world famous for fifteen minutes" as well as by the pop-art style of his works. The visible part of the installation consists of a digital camera and a flat-panel monitor dressed up like a precious painting (see figure 1 left). A computer behind the scene runs a software that detects human faces in visitors' images taken by the camera, graphically transforms them, and then displays them for fifteen seconds. The graphical transformation actually applied is randomly selected among the ones pre-defined by the artist. In such a case the classification label would differ for the dimension **processing contributors**, whose value would be: *artist*, since the kind of processing executed on the content of the IDA depends only on what artist has directly provided within the artwork itself.

Another real IDA similar to the above two ones is described in [5]: an installation where the self-image of the spectator is changed by randomly chosen pre-defined func-

Fig. 1. The installations *15 seconds of fame* (left), and *Sonic Onyx* (right)

tions whose specific input parameters are provided by the spectator itself. In such a case the classification label is: [**content provider**:*audience*, **processing dynamics**:*casual change*, **processing contributors**:*audience*].

Another real IDA is described in [1]: an installation receiving texts, images and sound files from its audience through their Bluetooth enabled handheld devices and converting them into sound compositions played through the seven loudspeakers located in seven arms of the sculpture (see figure 1 right). 3D sound effects are thus obtained in the space defined by the sculpture itself. The globe of the sculpture contains a lighting system changing light colors according to the different sounds it plays. The classification label for such an IDA is [**content provider**:*audience*, **processing dynamics**:*static*, **processing contributors**:*artist*].

Our classification overcomes the limitations of previously presented ones and explicitly targets IDAs by means of an approach that it is rooted on the standard input-process-output view used for discussing Information Systems. Hence our proposal considers interactivity just as one of the components of the classification and is therefore more balanced.

We have not considered in our classification scheme issues related to hardware and software, either in terms of IDA development environment or in terms of the environment where the work is viewed, since both these issues are too much dependent on the current state of development of technology. Hence the characterization of these aspects, while useful from an historical point of view, does not make much sense for the intended use of IDA classification.

The classification might anyhow be refined by taking into account also the sensory channels by means of which interaction between IDA and its users happens, but this will be subject of further work.

3   Comparison with Previous Frameworks

In this section we provide a comparison between our classification framework and the previous ones. The comparison is not easy, since previous classification frameworks were based on the various kinds of interaction, while we have taken the more general approach of the Information Systems view.

To make the reader able to better understand the comparison we first recall here below the definition of previous classes provided by the previous works in the literature.

Sommerer and Mignonneau [8] discuss two types of interaction:

Pre-Designed: the viewer can choose her path of interaction among a set of limited and pre-defined possibilities,

Evolutionary: the artwork's processes are linked to interaction and interaction is evolving continuously.

Hannington and Reed [4] distinguish three types of interaction:

Passive: the content has a linear presentation and the user interacts by only starting and stopping the presentation,

Interactive: the user is allowed to choose her personal path through the content,

Adaptive: the user is able to enter her own content and control how it is used.

Edmonds, Turner, and Candy [3] discuss four categories of "relationship between the artwork, artist, viewer and environment":

Static: there is no interaction,

Dynamic-Passive: the artwork response is triggered by environmental factors,

Dynamic-Interactive: the human presence and/or actions (purposeful or not) are used as parameters for changing the artwork, whose processing rules are static,

Dynamic-Interactive (varying): the processing rules used by artwork to change its output are modified by an agent (the artwork software or a human).

Table 1. Comparison with the previous classifications

		Content Provider			Processing Dynamics				Processing Contributors		
		Artist	Audience	Environment	Static	Predefined Change	Casual Change	Evolutionary Change	Self	Audience	Environment
[8]	Pre-designed	X	O		X	O			O	X	
	Evolutionary	X	X		O	X	X	X		X	O
[4]	Passive	X			X		O		X	O	
	Interactive	X	O		X		O			X	
	Adaptive		X			X	O			X	
[3]	Static	X			X				X		
	Dynamic-passive			X	X	O					X
	Dynamic-interactive		X		X	X				X	X
	Dynamic-interactive (varying)		X	X	X	X	X			X	X
	Int.Rules: Static				X						
	Int.Rules: Dynamic					X	X	X	O	O	
[9]	Tr.Par: Human Presence	O							O	X	
	Tr.Par: Human Action	O							O	X	
	Tr.Par: Environment			O					O		X
	Cont.Orig: Predefined by the Artist	X				O	O	O	X		
	Cont.Orig: Users Input		X		O					X	
	Cont.Orig: Generated / Algorithmic	O				O	O	X	X		

Trifonova, Jaccheri, and Bergaust [9] consider three categories, with various subdivisions:

Interaction Rules: whether the rules controlling the interaction are *static* (i.e., they never change during artwork's life) or *dynamic* (i.e., they may change),

Triggering Parameters: whether the interaction rules depend just on the *human presence*, or it is required some form of *human action*, or it is the *environment* that controls them,

Content Origin: whether what the artwork shows is *predefined by the artist*, or provided by the *user*, or *generated* by the software, possibly through some evolutionary *algorithm*.

The relation between previous classifications and ours is represented in table 1, where an X means that what was classified under the others' class labeling the row can be classified with our class labeling the column. An O means that the others' class labeling the row has some relevance to our class labeling the column.

4 Validation of the Proposed Framework

In this section we discuss how the IDAs analysed in [2] can be classified on the basis of the proposed framework.

Table 2. Installations considered for the validation of our classification

#	Installation Name	Author	Physical Interface for direct manipulation by the user	Input device(s)	Output device(s)
2	BMW Think Like No One	Studio DotDotDot	Mobile Phones	Camera, Mobil Phones	Videoprojector
8	FLAT/TRIX	Leonardo Betti	Table and objects	Camera	Lights, Speakers
9	Genova del Saper Fare	Studio EnneZeroTre	Torch	Camera	Videoprojectors
10	H:AND/RAYLS	Leonardo Betti		Camera	Videoprojector
13	If Shines	Leonardo Betti	Pipe	Microphone	Videoprojector, Speakers
14	Inconsapevoli Macchine Poetiche	Giacomo Verde	Keyboard and mouse	Keyboard	Computer display, Speakers
15	Interactive Collective Blu	Maurizio Bolognini	Mobile Phones	Mobile Phones	Videoprojector
16	Interno Neve	Giacomo Verde	Tulle curtain	Motion Sensors	Videoprojectors, Speakers
19	La cittá su misura	Studio EnneZeroTre		Camera	Videoprojector
31	Oracolo Ulisse	Studio Canali	Biomedical sensors	Pressure Sensors, Biomedical Sensors, Accelerometer	Videoprojector, Speakers
41	Sensual Zone	Federico Bucalossi	Arcade Videogame cabinet	Videogame controls	Videogame display, Headphones
42	SmellLink	Ennio Bertrand	Keyboard, Mouse	Keyboard, Mouse	Laser Printer
45	The Art of Italian Design	Studio EnneZeroTre	Torch	Camera	Videoprojector, Speakers
46	thevirtualgallery.org	Maurizio Bolognini	Keyboard, Mouse	Keyboard, Mouse	Videoprojector

In [2] a complete analysis of interactive art installations in Italy is provided, focusing on technological tools used by artist in the field. The analysis focused on the 54 installations for which there was enough available information, and they were classified according to the framework of [9]. Many of them received the same classification, hence we considered for our validation only one instance of each class identified during this classification process.

It is interesting to note that in [2] it is explicitly recognized a weakness of the framework of [9], since it is reported that all the 54 installations were classified as *static* under the dimension "interaction rules" of the framework of [9]. This means that such a dimension was useless to classify the installations since its values were not able to differentiate among installations.

We report in table 2 the most important descriptive data of one installation for each of the classes we have identified according to our framework. The number in the first column is the number by which installations are referred to in [2]. When the cell for the column "Physical Interface for direct manipulation by the user" is empty it means that the audience has no direct means for interacting with the IDA. Under the columns "Input Device(s)" and "Output Device(s)" we list the actual devices used by the IDA to, respectively, obtain data from the Audience or Environment and to produce data towards them.

In the table 3 we show how the installations listed in table 2 are classified according to our framework. When more than one value appears under some dimension this

Table 3. Classification of the considered installations

#	Content Provider	Processing Dynamics	Processing Contributors	Other Installations
8	artist	static	artist	21, 22, 23, 24, 28, 43, 44
10	artist	static	audience	3, 4, 11, 17, 18, 20, 25, 26, 35, 36, 39, 40, 47, 48, 49, 50, 51, 52, 53, 54
41	artist	PD/CC change	artist	6
16	artist	PD/CC change	audience	1, 7, 12, 27, 29, 32, 33, 34, 38
45	artist	static	artist environment	
19	artist	static	audience environment	
31	artist	PD/CC change	artist audience	
42	audience	static	artist	
46	audience	PD/CC change	artist	
15	audience	PD/CC change	audience	3, 30
14	artist audience	static	artist	
13	artist audience	PD/CC change	artist	37
2	artist audience	PD/CC change	audience	
9	artist environment	static	artist	

means the IDA has received more than one label. The value *PD/CC change* is used to represent both the labels *pre-defined change* and *casual change*, since [2] does not distinguish between them. As you can see, our classification does not have the above cited weakness of the classification defined in [9], since in all dimensions more than one value is used. We use all the labels, but for *evolutionary* in the dimension "Processing Dynamics". This was expected, since this kind of processing dynamics is very sophisticate in mathematical terms and also in [2] it is noted that no installations of this kind was found in Italy.

The last column lists the numbers of all other installations classified with the same set of labels. One class (the one in the second row) covers almost one half of all analyzed installations, and two other classes (first and fourth rows) cover about one third of them: this coarseness is shared with the classification in [9] and suggests it is of real practical importance to extend this work by distinguishing also among the various sensory channels by means of which interaction between IDA and its users happens.

Moreover, a further empirical validation of our classification needs to be done by directly interviewing the artists and getting their direct feedback on the new classification. Finally, the issues recalled in Section 1 in the research theme *Computer Art and the Commercial Perspective* are worth further investigations.

5   Conclusions

In this paper we have presented and discussed a novel framework for classification of interactive digital artworks (i.e., artworks based on ICT and where the user is directly involved in the production of the artistic output and called, for short, IDAs). The need for such a classification derives from the needs of relating and comparing homogeneous IDAs, of having a common description framework for researching, discussing and teaching about IDAs, and of definining "how-to" procedures for IDAs production and management.

We have built our classification framework on the basis of a critical revision and refinement of previous work. Its novelty lies in its being directly based on the input-process-output view considered for discussing Information Systems. Hence it allows to overcome weaknesses and limitations of the previous proposed ones. Our classification framework is validated by applying it to a set of 54 real-life examples of IDAs in Italy.

Acknowledgments. We would like to thank Letizia Jaccheri for useful and interesting discussions during the development of the work here described. Comments from referees helped in improving the presentation.

References

1. Ahmed, S.U., Jaccheri, L., M'kadmi, S.: Sonic Onyx: Case Study of an Interactive Artwork. In: Huang, F., Wang, R.-C. (eds.) ArtsIT 2009. LNICST, vol. 30, pp. 40–47. Springer, Heidelberg (2010),
   http://www.springerlink.com/content/
   nx243t25h1448750/fulltext.pdf

2. Cappellini, L.: Interactive installation art in Italy: an analytical survey. Master Degree Thesis in Informatics for Humanities, Supervisors: Luciana Vassallo and Letizia Jaccheri, University of Pisa (2009), http://www.idi.ntnu.no/~letizia/tesi_cappellini.pdf
3. Edmonds, E., Turner, G., Candy, L.: Approaches to interactive art systems. In: 2nd International Conference on Computer Graphics and Interactive Techniques in Australasia and South East Asia (GRAPHITE 2004), Singapore, pp. 113–117. ACM (2004)
4. Hannington, A., Reed, K.: Towards a taxonomy for guiding multimedia application development. In: 9th Asia-Pacific Software Engineering Conference (APSEC 2002), Gold Coast, Queensland, Australia (December 2002)
5. Nardelli, E.: A software based installation to assist self-reflection. In: 11th Consciousness Reframed International Research Conference (CR 2011), TEKS - Trondheim Electronic Arts Centre (November 2010)
6. Oates, B.J.: New frontiers for information systems research: Computer art as an information system. European Journal of Information Systems 15, 617–626 (2006)
7. Solina, F., Peer, P., Batagelj, B., Juvan, S.: 15 seconds of fame - an interactive computer-vision based art installation. In: 7th International Conference on Control, Automation, Robotics and Vision (ICARCV 2002), Singapore, pp. 198–204 (2002)
8. Sommerer, C., Mignonneau, L.: Art as a living system: Interactive computer artworks. Leonardo 32, 165–173 (2001)
9. Trifonova, A., Jaccheri, M.L., Bergaust, K.: Software engineering issues in interactive installation art. International Journal of Arts and Technology 1(1), 43–65 (2008)

Implementation of Adaptive Multimedia Application Concept in iDTV Environment

Filip Hanzl, Zdenek Mikovec, and Pavel Slavik

Faculty of Electrical Engineering, Czech Technical University in Prague, Czech Republic
{filip.hanzl,xmikovec,slavik}@fel.cvut.cz

Abstract. This paper describes a model of adaptation of multimedia application. The adaptation is based on user's progress in using a content of the application and a plan that defines long-time usage strategy of the application. The model was applied to education application but it can be used also in other use-cases. This model was designed to be easy to implement and use, and it is an alternative to robust learning models. The implementation of the model is presented on Physical Exercise application.

1 Introduction

Introduction of iDTV brought new HCI challenges coming from new user groups and new interactive environment. Nowadays the iDTV represents hybrid platform substituting television, personal computer and game consoles, and merges them together. From this perspective the iDTV content should be divided into three groups: (i) broadcast (in form of classic television), (ii) applications (similar to PC applications) and (iii) interactive multimedia applications (MA), which are combinations of both. The iDTV also offers several ways how to transfer content: (i) the broadcast brings the same content to all users, (ii) Internet Protocol television (IPTV) contains symmetric communication and it is able to transfer optional content to the user, (iii) a standalone application, independent of the content transfer, runs on user's iDTV device from its own data storage.

We have conducted a research of MAs and control of their content in iDTV environment, already for several years. We aim especially on education content (t-learning applications) [1]. Main problem we faced was an adaptation of the content according to user's progress in usage of MA. We were looking for simple model, which would define particular rules for control of the content. Related models based on personalized learning management system usually aim just on personalization and initial setting of MAs [2].

This work deals with an adaptation of MAs in iDTV environment. We have proposed a model of adaptive MA (AMA) independent of the way the content is transferred. Usage of this model is demonstrated on a Physical Exercise application developed in the framework of Vital Mind project [3].

F. Alvarez and C. Costa (Eds.): UCMEDIA 2010, LNICST 60, pp. 101–104, 2012.
© Institute for Computer Sciences, Social Informatics and Telecommunications Engineering 2012

2   Model of Adaptive Multimedia Application

We propose the model of AMA aimed on control of the content by user's progress during the work with the content. We also propose a formal description of the model. Components we use are partially transferable to SCORM [4] components.

Basic components of the content we are working with are multimedia content elements (MCE) that are similar to SCORM objects SCO. These elements are arranged into plans, which control the sequence of their execution. Plans are similar to SCORM sequencing. Finally we use rules for evaluation of user progress during the work with the content. All the control data are defined in XML files.

2.1   Multimedia Content Element

The multimedia content element has a form of video and is supplemented with an additional data. The additional data are divided according to the direction of an interaction and the synchronization with a video stream.

Synchronous content that contains information for the user is included in the video stream. While the content is being replayed, the synchronous data that are captured from the user as response to the content of the video stream are continuously evaluated. Finally a corresponding feedback is displayed to the user according to the evaluation rules. The feedback should be extended by an interactive questionnaire, which could be used for various purposes (e.g. to specify a reason of the user's failure). Integration of the additional content into the MCE is presented by the scheme in Fig. 1.

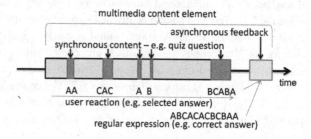

Fig. 1. Scheme of multimedia content element (MCE)

Synchronous content can be understood as a call for user interaction. A reaction to the content is expected in a form of key-press or set of key-presses. The key-presses are converted into characters and stored in captured string. When the playback of the multimedia content element finishes, the captured string is evaluated according to the predefined rules.

2.2   Plans and Rules

As it was mentioned above the MCEs are sorted into a plan. The plan represents the whole course where the multimedia application should take place. The plan is divided into several sessions, but real passing through the plan depends on the defined rules and their evaluation. Each session is created by one or more MCEs. When user starts the application for the first time, s/he enters the first session in the predefined plan. When the user successfully passes one session, s/he can start next session in the plan. On the other hand, when the user fails, s/he has to repeat current session (see Fig. 2).

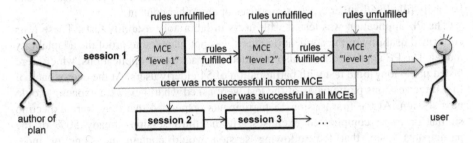

Fig. 2. Scheme of the model of AMA

The rules for evaluation of the synchronous content are formally defined by a regular expression which describes required behavior of the user. The regular expression is compared with string captured from an input device. The result of the comparison is an arithmetic variation defined as number of different characters between the regular expression and the captured string divided by the length of the regular expression. The variation is then compared with predefined tolerance value.

If the variation exceeds the tolerance, the plan is marked as unsuccessful and the user cannot proceed to the next MCE or session. The user has to try passing the MCE again until the variation is not lower than the tolerance. The repetition of one MCE may be annoying to the user. Therefore the tolerance is temporally increased (e.g. by 10%) for each additional trial in order to allow the user to reach other MCEs in the plan. This simplification enables the unsuccessful user to finish the session, but the session is still saved as unfulfilled and the user has to pass it again next time.

3   Implementation - Physical Exercise Application

Physical Exercise (PE) application is an iDTV application designed for elderly users. The application guides the user through series of physical exercises, which are demonstrated to the user in a form of video. The user has to repeat particular movements according to the video. The application uses special prototype of remote control that transfers user's movements into key-presses, which are captured by the application.

The implementation of the PE application is based on the model described in the previous chapter. It is implemented in Adobe Flash Lite 3.0, thus it can be used on different platforms including various types of iDTV devices. The definition of exercises, related regular expressions and training plan are stored in XML files.

The application starts the session according to the plan and particular exercises are shown. While the user is performing an exercise with the remote control in her/his hand, chars corresponding to particular movements are stored into a string. At the end of each exercise the captured string of movement chars is cómpared with the regular expression and evaluated. An appropriate feedback is then given to the user.

As all the data are located in XML files and video stream, the PE application can be easily filled with other types of exercises or any other content.

The PE application was tested with users in laboratory usability tests. These tests confirmed usability of the application, but it was not intended to proof the adaptability model. The PE application was also included in a package of applications, which were tested in the long-time test with participation of 54 elderly users. At the end of each of first three sessions participants of the test were asked what they were expecting to do next session. At the first session 18 participants responded that they were expecting similar or more complicated exercises. At the third session already 50% of the participants knew that the following session would contain the same or more complicated exercises according to their results. Although the model of the adaptation was not introduced to the participants they understood it relatively well.

4   Conclusion and Future Work

We have designed a model of AMA. The tool for AMA creation was implemented and used for implementation of the Physical Exercise application for iDTV. It can be also easily modified for other purposes.

In the future we will implement applications for other suitable use-cases based on our model. This can lead to further extensions of our model. These new use-cases can be for example language courses or educational quizzes similar to TV shows.

The other goal of future development of the model is to verify acceptance of the concept of adaptation by the users on different content than physical exercise. New long-time tests should be examined to analyze the users' acceptance of the adaptation provided by our model.

Acknowledgements. Research described in the paper was partially conducted within the framework of the Vital Mind project [3], funded by the European Commission.

References

1. Cmolik, L., Mikovec, Z., Slavik, P., Mannova, B.: Personalized e-learning in interactive digital television environment. In: IADIS Int. Conference WWW/Internet (2007)
2. Rey López, M., Meccawy, M., Brusilovsky, P., Díaz Redondo, R., Fernández Vilas, A., Ashman, H.: Resolving the Problem of Intelligent Learning Content in Learning Management Systems. International Journal on E-Learning 73 (2007)
3. Vital Mind Project: Research project number ICT-215387,
   http://www.vitalmindproject.eu
4. Advanced Distributed Learning: SCORM 2004, 4th edn. (2004),
   http://www.adlnet.gov/Technologies/scorm/default.aspx

Architectures for Future Media Internet

María Alduán[1], Federico Álvarez[1], Theodore Zahariadis[2], N. Nikolakis[2],
F. Chatzipapadopoulos[2], David Jiménez[1], and José Manuel Menéndez[1]

[1] E.T.S.I. Telecomunicación, U.P.M, Avda Complutense s/n, 28040 Madrid, Spain
{mam,fag,djb,jmm}@gatv.ssr.upm.es
[2] Synelixis Solution, P. Stavrou 5, 34100, Chalkida, Greece
{zahariad,nikolakis}@synelixis.com

Abstract. Among the major reasons for the success of the Internet have been
the simple networking architecture and the IP interoperation layer. However,
the traffic model has recently changed. More and more applications (e.g. peer-
to-peer, content delivery networks) target on the content that they deliver rather
than on the addresses of the servers who (originally) published/hosted that
content. This trend has motivated a number of content-oriented networking
studies. In this paper we summarize some the most important approaches.

Keywords: Content Centric, Future Media Internet architecture.

1 Introduction

Internet is today the most important information exchange mean and has become the
core communication environment not only for business relations, but also for social
and human interaction. Moreover, it is a common belief that the Internet is evolving
towards providing richer and more immersive experiences. Advances in video
capturing and creation will lead to massive creation of new multimedia content and
internet applications, including 3D videos, immersive environments, network gaming,
virtual worlds.

Among the major reasons for the success of the Internet have been the simple
networking architecture and the IP interoperation layer, which is so flexible as to
support a wide spectrum of applications. However, the original Internet architecture is
designed based on a client-server communication model. Every packet should have
the addresses of the endpoints (source and destination) to support host-to-host
applications like remote login and file transfer. However, the recent traffic
measurements reveal that more and more applications (e.g. peer-to-peer, content
delivery networks) target on the content that they deliver rather than the addresses of
the servers who (originally) published/hosted that content. This trend has motivated
content-oriented networking studies (e.g. DONA, CCNx).

In this paper we try to summarize some of the most important approaches in
Content Centric Internet, towards a Future Media Internet architecture model.

F. Alvarez and C. Costa (Eds.): UCMEDIA 2010, LNICST 60, pp. 105–112, 2012.

2   Future Media Internet Architecture Proposals

Before we analyze the various Future Media Internet proposals, let's review the relation between naming and routing. The current Internet focuses on the endpoints, thus, hosts are assigned (domain) names. Subsequently, content hosted in a server is characterized by the URL, which is the concatenation of the retrieval protocol, the host name and the path name. In order to fetch the content, the host (domain) name included in the URL has to be resolved to an IP address. So, the client application first retrieves the locator of the requested content (or more precisely, its holder) from a host name by looking up a database, DNS. Then the holding server is contacted to receive the content. Even though there is an additional layer of indirection (i.e. DNS lookup process), this lookup-by-name method has well served the Internet users with host-centric naming. Note that what is resolved it is not the individual contents, but the content holders.

In contrast, content-oriented networking designs hardly take hosts into account. Instead, content naming is used in routing directly, following the route-by name paradigm. In this paradigm, the content name is specified, the closest copy is located and dynamic routing is used to avoid the link/server failure. In terms of delivery efficiency, the route-by-name approach is more attractive since it can avoid the DNS lookup delay and will less likely waste time for servers out of service. However, the number of content files is orders of magnitude larger than the number of hosts. What is worse, it is difficult to aggregate the content names, while the locators (or addresses) of hosts are ready to be abstracted by a single identifier (i.e. a network prefix).

In the following we group different approaches towards the Future Media Internet architectures in those focused on the evolution of the current network architecture and those centered on its redesign. Both approaches aim to migrate "from the *where* to the *what*".

2.1   Content-Centric Network

One of the major candidates in content-centric networks is the CCNx approach proposed by Van Jacobson's *et. al.* [1]. This architecture targets the "*always available*" instead of the "*always on*" paradigm and the "*multiparty-to-multiparty information dissemination*" rather than traditional "*point-to-point conversations*". CCN is a purely content centric approach, based on named content/content chunks instead of named hosts.

CCN decouples content routing/forwarding, localization, security and content access, departing from IP in the critical way (Figure 1). CCN considers two packet types: Interest packets and Data packets. Content consumers request data by broadcasting their interests; interests are received by other nodes that, if they can satisfy them, respond with a Data packet. If not, they forward the interest packet via another network interface. As packets identify content, multiple nodes interested in the same information can share transmissions within the same medium by means of standard multicast suppression techniques [2].

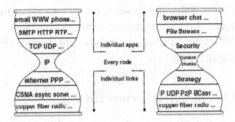

Fig. 1. CNN moves the universal component of the network stack from IP to chunks of named content [1]

Moreover, CCN architecture introduces three main data structures:

- FIB (*Forwarding Information Base*): used to forward interests towards potential sources of matching data.
- *Content Store*: the same as a buffer memory of an IP router but with a different replacement policy. IP packets belong to a point-to-point Communications so that once forwarded they are not useful anymore. On the other hand, all CCN packets are potentially useful for more than one consumer due to their idempotent nature. Unlike IP FIFO model, CCN allows data caching in intermediate network points
- PIT (*Pending Interest Table*): keep track of interests forwarded upstream towards content sources. These structures allow Data packets to return get to their requesters (it can be seen as a breadcrumb system

Similar to a URL path name, CNN naming follows a hierarchical structure (Figure 2) Each individual name in composed as a number of components that can be encrypted for privacy. The nature of this naming system allows different levels of granularity.

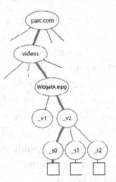

Fig. 2. Hierarchical Naming: Named Tree traversal

CCN architecture, includes evolutions of different mechanisms also present in IP networking such as: flow and congestion control, intra-domain and inter-domain routing, etc. Another feature of CCN is that the security resides in the data itself, not in the network channel as in today's Internet. Instead of focusing the security in the hosts and in communication links, it focuses security on encrypting the content itself. The network only concerns how to distribute the data and the publishers control the security of the data. As a consequence, it foresees the Future Internet network as a huge storage of authenticated data [1].

2.2   Data Oriented Network Architecture (DONA)

Instead of a hierarchical naming system that inherits from current IP model, DONA (Data Oriented Network Architecture) [4] is focused in naming and name resolution using flat names. DONA proposes a strict separation between naming and name resolution so that persistence, availability and authenticity problems can be solved. Persistence and authenticity problems are solved by the use of flat self-certifying names [4][5][6]. Availability problem is solved by the name resolution technique applied.

This resolution technique is based on the route-by-name paradigm so that a new entity called Resolution Handler (RH) appears. RHs, by interpreting the basic primitives FIND and REGISTER, are able to route content requests and responses. To support these two primitives, DONA introduces resolution handlers, which forward content to the users in an overlay manner. DONA names are flat, long and user unfriendly; so users will not have to remember these names directly, they will have their private human-readable name spaces [8] and rely on reliable external mechanisms such as search engines, recommender services, etc. for name resolution.

These flat self-certifying names are not new in the scientific community, it can also be found in TRIAD [6], HIP [7] and SFS [5]. The role this naming system can take in generic network architectures has been discussed in [9][10][11], which, as DONA, are focused in both, naming and name resolution.

2.3   Publish/Subscribe for Internet Perspective (PSIRP)

PSIRP (Publish/Subscribe for Internet Perspective) [13], [14] advocates for a new redesign of the network by means of a pub/sub approach. Just like DONA, PSIRP approach can be considered as semantically similar to a publish/subscribe (pub/sub) interface. PSIRP however aims to prevent SPAM or DoF attacks by living the control of the Communications to the information receivers.

PSIRP considers 4 identifiers in order to refer data chunks [12]: Application Identifiers (AId), Rendezvous Identifiers (RId), Scope Identifiers (SId) and Forwarding Identifiers (FId). RIds and SIds are self-certified names, so that, the same as in DONA, authenticity and integrity is guaranteed.

PSIRP architecture consists of autonomous systems called domains. These domains have at least three kind of nodes:

- *Topology Nodes (TN)*: in charge of the intra-domain topology, load balance between BNs and routing vector interchange among different domains (in a similar way as BGP)
- *Branching Nodes (BN)*: responsible of subscription messages routing and popular content caching

- *Forwarding Nodes (FN)*: implement a simple, cheap and fast forwarding algorithm by using a Bloom filter [15]
- *Rendezvous Points* are used to locate Publications within the network; these entities form rendezvous points Networks globally connected by hierarchical DHTs [16]. This aggregation enlarges system scalability.

For security purposes, PSIRP uses elliptic curve cryptography [17] and packet level authentication [18].

Similar to PSIRP, Scalable Internet Event Notification Architectures (Siena) [12] features a generic scalable publish/subscribe event-notification service. Siena formulates a general model of content-based addressing and routing to maximize both expressiveness and scalability.

2.4   Evolutionary FI Architecture (EFIA)

Assuming a progressive, rather than aggressive evolution towards Future Internet, the Future Content Networks (FCN) [19] group has proposed the EFIA architecture that consists of different virtual hierarchies of nodes (overlays, clouds or virtual groups of nodes), with different functionality (Figure 3). This model may be easily scaled to multiple levels of hierarchy (even mesh instantiations, where nodes may belong in more than one layers) and multiple variations, based on the available level of information and service delivery requirements and constrains.

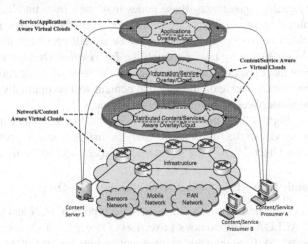

Fig. 3. Logical Future Content-Centric Internet Architecture

At the lower layer, it is the *Service/Network Provider Infrastructure*. Users are connected to the infrastructure as content producers and consumers (Prosumers). Content will be routed, assuming basic quality requirements and if possible cached to some degree in this layer. Progressively this overlay will be reduced or even eliminated.

The Infrastructure should, on the one hand, hide all unnecessary complexity (e.g. physical network topology, mobile terminal handover) and on the other hand provide all the necessary information, so that more intelligent nodes will take all necessary decisions in order to support the required functionality (including guaranteeing the QoS).

The medium layer is the *Distributed Content/Services Aware Overlay*. Content-Aware Network Nodes (e.g. core routers, edge routers, home gateways, terminal devices) will be located at this overlay. These nodes will have the intelligence to filter the content and Web services that flow through them (e.g. via Deep Packet Inspection, DPI) or identify streaming sessions and traffic (e.g. via signalling analysis). Alternatively, the content may be considered formulating *information objects* as first order elements in the network, thus be directly identifiable by the network nodes. In either case, the Nodes of this group will recognise and qualify the content. Part of this information may be stored locally and/or reported to the higher layer of hierarchy (Information Overlay).

Content/Services Aware Overlay may be dynamically constructed at the layers between the content and the information overlays. We may consider overlays for content caching, content classification (even content indexing in the future), network monitoring, content adaptation, optimal delivery/streaming. With respect to content delivery, nodes at this layer may operate as hybrid client-server, peer-to-peer or cloud networks, according to the delivery requirements.

At a higher layer, it is the *Information Overlay*. It will consist of intelligent nodes or servers that have a distributed knowledge of both the content/web-service location/caching and the (mobile) network instantiation/conditions. Based on the actual network deployment and instantiation, the service scenario, the service requirements and the service quality agreements, these nodes may vary from unreliable peers in a next-P2P topology to secure corporate routers or even data centers in distributed carrier-grade cloud networks. The content may be stored/ cached at the *Information Overlay* or at lower hierarchy layers, though the *Information Overlay* will be always aware of the content/services location/caching and the network information. Based on this information, it may decide on the way that content will be optimally retrieved and delivered to the subscribers or inquiring users or services.

Finally, at the highest layer the *Application's layer* is located. Applications will use efficiently the services, the information and the media/content provided by the content-centric architecture and offer novel media experiences to the users.

2.5   Autonomic Layer-Less Object Architecture (ALLOA)

Moving from an evolutionary to a more clean-slate approach, FCN and [20] introduce the concept of ALLOA (Autonomous Layer-Less Object Architecture) based on the "Content Objects". A Content Object (or simply object) is a polymorphic/holistic container, which may consist of media, rules, behaviour, relations and characteristics or any combination of the above.

- *Media: anything that a human can perceive/experience with his/her senses*
- *Characteristics:* meaningfully description of the object.
- *Rules:* can refer to the way an object is treated and manipulated by other objects or the environment (discovered, retrieved, casted, adapted, delivered, transformed, presented)

- *Behaviour:* can refer to the way the object affects other objects or the environment
- *Relations:* between an object with other objects can refer to time, space, synchronization issues

Objects can be hierarchically organized, like the constituting instrument channels of a music band, and can trigger the generation of new objects. An object can be divided/ spit into new objects or multiple objects can be combined/merged and finally create new objects, and these operations may happen while travelling over the network. Also an object can be cloned. The clone keeps the characteristics of its "parent" object but knows that it is a clone.

The autonomous objects will travel over the network, split and combined to generate the new service or virtual world object. The Future Content Centric Internet will support the content objects in order to meet their relations.

More specifically, transfer and integration of objects for the purpose of the creation of an orchestrated "Media" experience clearly demands intelligence that combines application ("Service/Media") and "Content" information. The intelligence could be embedded in the objects themselves, retrieving information from the network and providing instructions for routing and transformation, or the intelligence could be hosted in network nodes that attempt to satisfy the requests of the objects as they are described in the "Rules", "Behaviours" and "Relationships" (which take input from the "Information/Adaptation", "Content" and "Infrastructure" layers) . Finally, the "Characteristics" that meaningfully describe an object take, mainly, input from the "Information/Adaptation" layer.

3   Conclusions

Among the major reasons for the success of the Internet have been the simple networking architecture and the IP interoperation layer, which is so flexible as to support a wide spectrum of applications. However, the recent traffic measurements reveal that more and more applications target on the content that they deliver rather than the addresses of the servers who (originally) published/hosted that content.

In this paper we summarized some of the most important approaches towards a Future Media Internet architecture model. As this is a very hot-topic world-wide, this can't be an extensive list. However, it is obvious that there are many new ideas that have to be tested /evaluated towards efficiency, scalability, backwards compatibility and security before we can safely and realistically remove IP from Internet.

Acknowledgement. This paper is partially based on the EC funded projects nextMedia (ICT-249065) and COAST (ICT-248036) and the work that has taken place at the European Commission Future Content Networks Group (FCN), and the Future Media Internet Architecture Think Tank (FMIA-TT), supported by the project nextMEDIA.

References

1. Jacobson, V., Smetters, D., Thornton, J., Plass, M., Briggs, N., Braynard, R.: Networking Named Content. In: Proceeding of ACM CoNEXT 2009, Rome, Italy (December 2009)
2. Palo Alto Research Center, Content-centric network, http://www.ccnx.com/
3. Adamson, B., Bormann, C., Handley, M., Macker, J.: Multicast Negative-Acknowledgement (NACK) Building Blocks. IETF, RFC 5401 (November 2008)
4. Koponen, T., Chawla, M., Chun, B.-G., Ermolinskiy, A., Kim, K.H., Shenker, S., Stoica, I.: A Data-Oriented (and Beyond) Network Architecture. In: SIGCOMM (2007)
5. Mazi'eres, D., Kaminsky, M., Kaashoek, M.F., Witchel, E.: Separating Key Management from File System Security. In: Proc. of SOSP 1999, pp. 124–139, Charleston, SC, USA (December 1999)
6. Gritter, M., Cheriton, D.R.: TRIAD: A New Next-Generation Internet Architecture (July 2000), http://www-dsg.stanford.edu/triad
7. Moskowitz, R., Nikander, P.: Host Identity Protocol Architecture. RFC 4423, IETF (May 2006)
8. Ford, B., Strauss, J., Lesniewski-Laas, C., Rhea, S., Kaashoek, F., Morris, R.: Persistent Personal Names for Globally Connected Mobile Devices. In: Proc. of OSDI 2006, Seattle, WA, USA, pp. 233–248 (November 2006)
9. Balakrishnan, H., Lakshminarayanan, K., Ratnasamy, S., Shenker, S., Stoica, I., Walfish, M.: A Layered Naming Architecture for the Internet. In: Proc. of ACM SIGCOMM 2004, Portland, OR, USA, pp. 343–352 (August 2004)
10. Walfish, M., Balakrishnan, H., Shenker, S.: Untangling the Web from DNS. In: Proc. of NSDI 2004, San Francisco, CA, USA, pp. 225–238 (March 2004)
11. Walfish, M., Stribling, J., Krohn, M., Balakrishnan, H., Morris, R., Shenker, S.: Middleboxes No Longer Considered Harmful. In: Proc. of OSDI 2004, San Francisco, CA, USA, pp. 215–230 (December 2004)
12. Siena (Content-based Network), http://wwwserl.cs.colorado.edu/carzanig/siena/
13. Lagutin, D., Visala, K., Tarkoma, S.: Publish/Subscribe for Internet: PSIRP Perspective. In: Tselentis, G., et al. (eds.) Towards the Future Internet – A European Research Perspective, pp. 75–85. IOS Press (2010)
14. Tarkoma, et al.: The Publish/Subscribe Internet Routing Paradigm (PSIRP): Designing the Future Internet Architecture. In: Tselentis, G., et al. (eds.) Towards the Future Internet – A European Research Perspective, pp. 102–111. IOS Press (2009)
15. Jokela, P., Zahemszky, A., Esteve, C., Arianfar, S., Nikander, P.: LIPSIN: Line Speed Publish/Subscribe Inter-Networking. In: Proceeding of SIGCOMM 2009, Barcelona, Spain (August 2009)
16. Ganesan, P., Gummadi, K., Garcia-Molina, H.: Canon in G Major: Designing DHTs with Hierarchical Structure. In: ICDCS 2004, pp. 263–272 (2004)
17. Miller, V.S.: Use of Elliptic Curves in Cryptography. In: Williams, H.C. (ed.) CRYPTO 1985. LNCS, vol. 218, pp. 417–426. Springer, Heidelberg (1986)
18. Lagutin, D.: Redesigning Internet – The packet level authentication architecture. Licentiate's thesis, Helsinki University of Technology, Finland (June 2008)
19. FCN: Why do we need a Content-Centric Future Internet? Proposals towards Content-Centric Internet Architectures, Prague (May 2009)
20. Zahariadis, T., Daras, P., Bouwen, J., Niebert, N., Griffin, D., Álvarez, F., Camarillo, G.: Towards a Content-Centric Internet. In: Tselentis, G., et al. (eds.) Towards the Future Internet – A European Research Perspective, pp. 227–236. IOS Press (2010)

Multi-sensored Vision for Autonomous Production of Personalized Video Summaries

Fan Chen, Damien Delannay, and Christophe De Vleeschouwer

ICTEAM, Université catholique de Louvain, Belgium
{damien.delannay,christophe.devleeschouwer}@uclouvain.be

Abstract. Democratic and personalized production of multimedia content is a challenge for content providers. In this paper, members of the FP7 APIDIS consortium explain how it is possible to address this challenge by building on computer vision tools to automate the collection and distribution of audiovisual content. In a typical application scenario, a network of cameras covers the scene of interest, and distributed analysis and interpretation of the scene are exploited to decide what to show or not to show about the event, so as to edit a video from of a valuable subset of the streams provided by each individual camera. Generation of personalized summaries through automatic organization of stories is also considered. In final, the proposed technology provides practical solutions to a wide range of applications, such as personalized access to local sport events through a web portal, cost-effective and fully automated production of content for small-audience, or automatic log in of annotations.

Keywords: Automatic production, personalized summarization, multi-camera.

1   Introduction

This Today's media consumption evolves towards increased user-centric adaptation of contents, to meet the requirements of users having different expectations in terms of story-telling and heterogeneous constraints in terms of access devices. To address such kind of demands, this paper presents a unified framework for cost-effective and autonomous generation of sport team video contents from multi-sensored data. It first investigates the automatic extraction of intelligent contents from a network of sensors distributed around the scene at hand. Here, intelligence refers to the identification of salient segments within the audiovisual content, using distributed scene analysis algorithms. Second, it will explain how that knowledge can be exploited to automate the production and personalize the summarization of video contents.

In more details, salient segments in the raw video content are identified based on player movement analysis and scoreboard monitoring. Player detection and tracking methods rely on the fusion of the foreground likelihood information computed in each view, which allows overcoming the traditional hurdles associated to single view analysis, such as occlusions, shadows and changing illumination. Scoreboard monitoring provides valuable additional inputs to recognize the main actions of the

F. Alvarez and C. Costa (Eds.): UCMEDIA 2010, LNICST 60, pp. 113–122, 2012.

game. To produce semantically meaningful and perceptually comfortable video summaries based on the extraction of sub-images from the raw content, our proposed framework introduces three fundamental concepts, i.e. "completeness", "smoothness" and "fineness", to abstract the semantic and narrative requirement of video contents. We formulate the selection of temporal segments and corresponding viewpoints in the edited summary as two independent optimization problems that aim at maximizing individual user preferences (e.g. in terms of preferred player or video access resolution), given the outcomes of scene analysis algorithms. We refer to the research outputs of the FP7 APIDIS research project to demonstrate our framework.

2   Player Tracking and Sport Action Understanding

This section explains how multi-view analysis can support team sport actions monitoring and understanding. It first surveys our solution for players detection and tracking, as required by autonomous production tools. It then presents how those data are completed by the scoreboard information to recognize the main actions of a basket-ball game, so as to support personalized summarization.

2.1   Multi-view Player Detection, Recognition, and Tracking

Tracking multiple people in cluttered and crowded scenes is a challenging task, primarily due to occlusion between people. The problem has been extensively studied, mainly because it is common to numerous applications, ranging from (sport) event reporting to surveillance in public space. Detailed reviews of tracking research in monocular or multi-view contexts are for example provided in Khan and Shah [6] or Fleuret et al. [5]. Since all players have similar appearance in a team sport context, we focus on methods that do not use color models or shape cues of individual people, but instead rely on the distinction of foreground from background in each individual view to infer the ground plane locations that are occupied by people. Those methods are reviewed in Delannay et al. [4].

Similar to [5],[6], our approach computes foreground likelihood independently on each view, using standard background modeling techniques. It then fusions those likelihoods by projecting them on the ground plane, thereby defining a set of so-called ground occupancy masks (see Fig.1). The originality of our method compared to previous art is twofold. First, it computes the ground occupancy mask in a computationally efficient way, based on the implementation of integral image techniques on a well-chosen transformed version of the foreground silhouettes. Second, it proposes an original and simple greedy heuristic to handle occlusions, and alleviate the false detections occurring at the intersection of the masks projected from distinct players' silhouettes by distinct views. In final, our method appears to improve the state of the art both in terms of computational efficiency and detection reliability, reducing the error rate by one order of magnitude, typically from 10 to 1%. Due to the lack of space, we encourage the interested reader to access the description presented in [4] for more details. Once players and referee have been localized, histogram analysis is performed to assign a team label to each detection (see bounding boxes color in Fig. 1). Further segmentation and analysis of the regions composing the expected body area permits to detect and recognize the digit(s) printed on the players' shirts when they face the camera [4].

Fig. 1. Players detection&recognition: On the left, the foreground likelihoods are extracted in each view. They are projected to define a ground occupancy map, from which people positions are extracted through an occlusion-aware greedy process.

Since the player digit can only be read when the player's back faces one of the cameras, we have to track the detected players across time. Therefore, we propagate tracks over a 1-frame horizon, based on the Munkres general assignment algorithm [7]. Gating is used to prevent unlikely matches. A high level analysis module is also used to link together partial tracks based on shirt color and/or player digit estimation.

2.2 Event Recognition

This section summarizes how to detect and recognize the main actions occurring during a basketball game, i.e. field goals, violations, fouls, balls out-of-bounds, free-throws, throw-in, throw, rebounds, and lost balls. All those actions correspond to 'clock-events', i.e. they cause a stop, start or re-initialization of the 24" clock. Hence, we assume an accurate monitoring of the 24" clock, and of the scoreboard, and propose to organize the actions hierarchically, as a function of the observed clock and scoreboard status. This results in the tree structure depicted in Fig. 2 and 3. Most of the tests implemented in the nodes of the tree only rely on the clock and scoreboard information. When needed, this information is completed by visual hints, typically provided as outcomes of the players (and ball) tracking algorithms. The initial

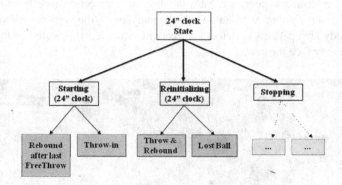

Fig. 2. Basket-ball action tree structure

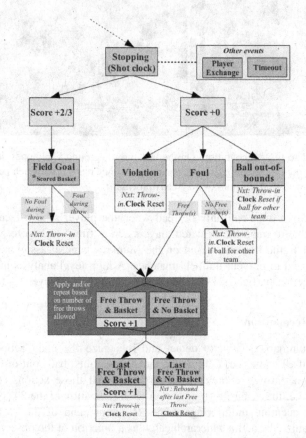

Fig. 3. Basket-ball actions tree structure

instance of our system defines dedicated 'if-then-else' rules to decide about the branch to go in each node. As an example, the decision to take after a start of the 24'' clock - on the left node of Fig. 2 - about a 'rebound' or 'throw-in' action can be inferred from the analysis of the trajectories of the players. A detailed description of the detectors involved in the nodes of this tree is beyond the scope of this paper, and can be accessed in Devaux et al. [9]. The approach achieves above 90 % accuracy.

3   Autonomous Production of Personalized Video Summaries

To produce condensed video reports of a sport event, the temporal segments corresponding to actions that are worth being included in the summary have to be selected. For each segment, local story organization and selection of appropriate viewpoints to render the scene are also essential. In an autonomous system, all those steps have to be run in an integrated manner, independently of any human intervention. This section describes how to design and integrate video analysis, production, and summarization technologies to automate and personalize the generation of video summaries in a team sport environment, using a distributed set of cameras.

3.1   Problem and Solution Overview

Although the perception of a production strategy is subjective and relative to individual's perspective, there is a set of general principles whose implementation results in improved and more enjoyable viewing experience. In our proposed framework, we identify three factors affecting the quality of the produced content, and interpret production and summarization as optimization processes that trade-off among these three factors. In more details, the factors are defined as follows:

- **Completeness** stands for both the integrity of view rendering in camera/viewpoint selection, and that of story-telling in summarization. A viewpoint of high completeness includes more salient objects, while a complete summary includes more key actions.
- **Smoothness** refers to the graceful displacement of the virtual camera viewpoint, and to the continuous story-telling resulting from the selection of contiguous temporal segments. Preserving smoothness is important to avoid distracting the viewer from the story by abrupt changes of viewpoints or constant temporal jumps, see Owens [8].
- **Fineness** refers to the amount of details provided about the rendered action. Spatially, it favors close views. Temporally, it implies redundant story-telling, including replays. Increasing the fineness of a video does not only improve the viewing experience, but is also essential in guiding the emotional involvement of viewers by close-up shots.

Obviously, those three concepts have to be maximized to produce a meaningful and visually pleasant content. In practice however, maximization of the three concepts often results in antagonist decisions, under some limited resource constraints, typically expressed in terms of the spatial resolution and temporal duration of the produced content. For example, at fixed output video resolution, increasing completeness generally induces larger viewpoints, which in turns decreases fineness of salient objects. Similarly, increased smoothness of viewpoint movement prevents accurate pursuit of actions of interest along the time. The same observations hold regarding the selection of segments and the organization of stories along the time, under some global duration constraints.

Hence, our production/summarization system turns to search for a good balance between the three major factors. Our methods described in Chen and De Vleeschouwer [1-3] first define quantitative metrics to reflect completeness, fineness, and closeness. They then formulate constrained optimization problems to balance those concepts. Interestingly, it appears that both the metrics and the problem can be formulated as a function of individual user preferences, typically expressed in terms of output video resolution, or preferred camera or players' actions, so that it becomes possible to personalize the produced content.

In addition, for improved computational efficiency, both production and summarization are envisioned in the divide and conquer paradigm. This especially makes sense since video contents intrinsically have a hierarchical structure, starting from each frame, shots (set of consecutive frames created from similar viewpoints), to semantic segments (consecutive shots logically related to the same action), and ending with the overall sequence.

Figure 4 summarizes the framework resulting from the above considerations. The event timeframe is first cut into semantically meaningful temporal segments, such as an offense/defense round of team sports. For each segment, several narrative options are considered. Each option defines a local story, which consists of multiple shots with different camera coverage. Benefits and costs are then assigned to each local story. The cost simply corresponds to the duration of the story. The benefit reflects user satisfaction (under some individual preferences[1]), and measures how some general requirements, e.g., the continuity and completeness of the story, are fulfilled. Those pairs of benefits and costs are then fed into the summarization engine, which solves a conventional resource allocation problem to find the organization of local stories that achieves the highest benefit under the constrained summary length.

Interestingly, a local story not only includes shots to render the global action at hand, but also shots for explanative and decorative purposes, e.g., replays and close-up views. For some of our previous work [3] that consider the summarization of content released by the production room, shots are simply defined based on shot boundary detection algorithms, while segments results from view type sequence monitoring. Alternatively, our proposed framework also supports the autonomous selection of viewpoints to render the action, based on a set of cameras covering the scene. In that particular case, segments and shots are defined based on scene interpretation (i.e. action recognition), and the viewpoint sequence associated to each shot is computed automatically, taking into account the nature of the shots (close-up view, replay, etc) composing the narrative option, and the position of objects-of-interest, as defined by video analysis modules.

---

[1] This might involve video analysis, to measure the consistency between users preferences, and actual content of the scene.

In the sequel, our framework for automatic selection of viewpoints is presented. This autonomous production framework directly relies on the knowledge of players' positions. Due to space limitation, we omit the description of the summarization resource allocation framework, but refer interested readers to our paper [3] for a detailed description.

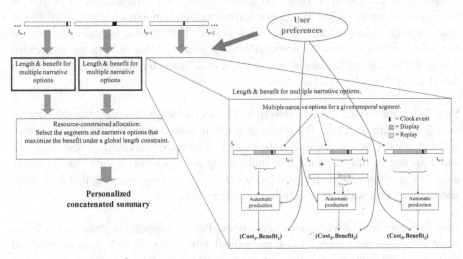

Fig. 4. Automatic Production in Divide-and-conquer Paradigm

3.2 Viewpoint Selection for Team Sport Videos

In this section, we review our method for automatic production of video content, to render an action involving one or several players and/or objects of interest. Whilst extendable to other contexts (e.g. PTZ camera control), the process has been designed to select which fraction of which camera view should be cropped in a distributed set of still cameras to render the scene at hand in a semantically meaningful and visually

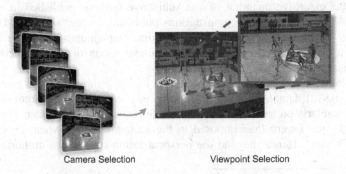

Camera Selection   Viewpoint Selection

Fig. 5. Camera selection and field of view selection

pleasant way. Formal description and extensive validation of the method are provided in [1],[2]. Here, we present an intuitive description of the approach depicted in Fig. 5. Given the positions of the objects of interest, the process proceeds in three steps.

Step 1: Camera-Wise Field of View Selection. At each time instant and in each view, this stage selects the cropping parameters that optimize the trade-off between completeness and fineness. Here, the completeness counts the number of players in the displayed image, while the fineness measures the amount of pixels available to describe each object of interest, i.e. each player. The purpose is here to select the field-of-view that renders the scene of interest in a way that (allows the viewer to) follow the action carried out by the multiple and interacting players that have been detected, e.g. by video analysis tools.

Step 2: Frame-Wise Camera Selection. The second stage considers the selection of the right camera to render the action at a given time instant. It rates the viewpoint selected in each view according to the quality of its completeness/closeness trade-off, and to its degree of occlusions. The highest rate corresponds to a view that (i) makes most object of interest visible, and (ii) is close to the action, meaning that it presents important objects with lots of details, i.e. a high resolution.

Step 3: Smoothing of Viewpoint Sequences. For the temporal segment at hand, this stage computes the parameters of an optimal virtual camera that pans, zooms and switches across views to preserve high ratings of selected viewpoints while minimizing the amount of virtual camera movements. The purpose is to build the edited video by selecting and concatenating video segments provided by multiple cameras, in a way that promotes the informative cameras, while avoiding perceptually inopportune switching between cameras and/or abrupt viewpoint changes. More details about the smoothing process are available in [1],[2].

4   Experimental Results

Space limitation prevents us to include experimental results in the paper. We refer the reader to the extensive quantitative and subjective analysis published in our recent papers [1-4], but also to the demonstrations published on the web [10]. During the conference, we plan to demonstrate our real-time implementation of the integrated prototype for personalized production and summarization of pre-recorded and pre-analyzed basket-ball games.

Interestingly, the subjective experiments run based on the production component of this prototype [2] demonstrate that the viewpoints selected by the automatic virtual director is regularly preferred to the ones selected by a human producer. This is partly explained by the severe load imposed to the human operator when the number of camera increases[2]. Hence, beyond the personalization capabilities authorized by the

---

[2] In conventional systems, the load is split between several cameramen (one per camera), and one or several producers (each one selecting the best view among a subset of the cameras).

possibility to repeat the automatic process with different parameters, the present framework also alleviates the bottleneck experienced by a human operator, when jointly and simultaneously processing a large number of source cameras.

5   Conclusions

The framework presented in this paper for producing personalized video summaries has been designed to offer four major advantages. Namely, it offers 1.) Strong personalization opportunities. Semantic clues about the events detected in the scene can easily be taken into account to adapt camerawork or story organization to the needs of the users. 2.) Story-telling complying with production principles. On the one hand, production cares about smooth camera movement while capturing the essence of team actions. On the other hand, summarization naturally favors continuous and complete local stories. 3) Computational efficiency. We adopt a divide-and-conquer strategy and consider a hierarchical processing, from frames to action segments. 4) Generic and flexible deployment capabilities. The proposed framework balances the benefits and costs of different production strategies, where benefits and other narrative options can be defined in many ways, depending on the application context.

Acknowledgments. The author would like to thank the APIDIS partners for their support in the acquisition of the video material exploited in this work. They also thank the European Commission and the Walloon Region for funding part of this work through the FP7 APIDIS and WIST2 WALCOMO projects, respectively.

References

1. Chen, F., De Vleeschouwer, C.: Autonomous production of basket-ball videos from multi-sensored data with personalized viewpoints. In: The 10th International Workshop for Multimedia Interactive Services, London, UK, pp. 81–84 (2009)
2. Chen, F., De Vleeschouwer, C.: Personalized production of team sport videos from multi-sensored data under limited display resolution. Computer Vision and Image Understanding. Special Issue on Sensor Fusion 114(6), 667–680 (2009)
3. Chen, F., De Vleeschouwer, C.: A resource allocation framework for summarizing team sport videos. In: IEEE International Conference on Image Processing, Cairo, Egypt, pp. 4349–4352 (2009)
4. Delannay, D., Danhier, N., De Vleeschouwer, C.: Detection and recognition of sports (wo)men from multiple views. In: 3rd ACM/IEEE International Conference on Distributed Smart Cameras, Como, Italy (2009)
5. Fleuret, F., Berclaz, J., Lengagne, R., Fua, P.: Multi-camera people tracking with a probabilistic occupancy map. IEEE Transactions on Pattern Analysis and Machine Intelligence 30(2), 267–282 (2008)
6. Khan, S.M., Shah, M.: Tracking multiple occluding people by localizing on multiple scene planes. IEEE Trans. on Pattern Analysis and Mach. Intel. 31(3), 505–519 (2009)
7. Munkres, J.: Algorithms for the assignment and transportation problems. SIAM J. Control 5, 32–38 (1957)

8. Owens, J.: Television sports production, 4th edn. Focal Press, Burlington (2007)
9. Devaux, F.-O., Delannay, D., De Vleeschouwer, C.: Autonomous production of images based on distributed and intelligent sensing. In: Event Detection Algorithms' Public Deliverable of the FP7 APIDIS Project (2010),
http://www.apidis.org/publications.htm
10. APIDIS website, http://www.apidis.org including some preliminary results presented during IBC 2009 (2009),
http://thetis.tele.ucl.ac.be/Apidis/chen/www/
results-ibc2009.html

Efficient Video Indexing on the Web: A System That Crowdsources User Interactions with a Video Player

Ioannis Leftheriotis, Chrysoula Gkonela, and Konstantinos Chorianopoulos

Ionian Univesity, Department of Informatics, 7 Tsirigoti square, 49100 Corfu, Greece
{c09levth,c09gkon,choko}@ionio.gr

Abstract. In this paper, we propose a user-based video-indexing method, that automatically generates thumbnails of the most important scenes of an online video stream, by analyzing users' interactions with a web video player. As a test bench to verify our idea we have extended the YouTube video player into the VideoSkip system. In addition, VideoSkip uses a web-database (Google Application Engine) to keep a record of some important parameters, such as the timing of basic user actions (play, pause, skip). Moreover, we implemented an algorithm that selects representative thumbnails. Finally, we populated the system with data from an experiment with nine users. We found that the VideoSkip system indexes video content by crowdsourcing implicit users interactions, such as pause and thirty seconds skip. Our early findings point toward improvements of the web video player and its thumbnail generation technique. The VideoSkip system could compliment content-based algorithms, in order to achieve efficient video-indexing in difficult videos, such as lectures or sports.

Keywords: Video, Indexing, Thumbnails, Pragmatics, Semantics, crowdsourcing.

1   Introduction

During the last years, the intense growth of the internet has given impetus to sharing of video material between users all over the world. Nowadays, User Generated Content together with movies, tv series, lectures, sports video, news etc., are all available to the public. One of the most successful platforms that millions of users use on a daily basis in order to browse all these videos is YouTube.

Users, apart from watching videos on the main YouTube video player, can upload videos or perform other important tasks, such as commenting videos, replying with other videos, tagging or publishing videos in other platforms. A lot of research has been done so as to prove the importance of the comments and other metadata information for complex processes, such as generating important thumbnails of the video or even producing automatically generated summaries. But, although there is a variety of methods that collect and manipulate all these information, the majority of them is usually burdensome for the users. Moreover, the percentage of users leaving a comment is too small according to the real number of viewers of a video.

F. Alvarez and C. Costa (Eds.): UCMEDIA 2010, LNICST 60, pp. 123–131, 2012.
© Institute for Computer Sciences, Social Informatics and Telecommunications Engineering 2012

In this work, we suggest the idea that the best way to extract useful information about a video, is to simply let the viewer browse the video as if he was in the YouTube web player, and just store all the interactions with the player (e.g. play, pause) for future use. As Shamma et al[8] proved, the more the emotive energy of a scene, the more the specific interval of the video containing that scene is used. Combining that result with the fact that we are proposing to record all the interactions between the user and the web player in order to infer the most important scenes of a video, and to automatically generate thumbnails, or even implement a summarization feature.

Bearing this perspective in mind, we implemented a web video player based on the YouTube API (application programming interface) and we linked it with a small database by using Google APP Engine infrastructure. In the remaining of the paper, apart from presenting the web video player, we examine the properties that this player should have, discussed some considerations about the video content of the player, and finally, we present the results of a pilot usability test we conducted with 9 subjects.

2   Related Work

A lot of research has been done in order to improve users' browsing experience while watching video content. Some researchers use automated summarization techniques. Takahashi et al[10] for example, propose a summarization method for sports video that uses metadata to extract the important video segments. Sports video are being processed beforehand and information such as play ranks, play occurrence time and number of replays are used to generate a video summary whose duration is selected by the user.

Another technique for improving browsing experience is using methods that generate thumbnails. For example, SmartSkip[1] from Microsoft Research is an interface that uses the histogram of images in almost every 10 seconds of the video and looking at rapid overall changes in the color and brightness, generates thumbnails. Li, Gupta et al[5]developed an interface that generates shot boundaries using a detection algorithm that identifies transitions between shots. Although the table of contents of the video is pre-generated, they use techniques such as time compression (increase playback speed) and pause removal (detects and removes pauses and silence segments of the video) that help the user browse the video more efficiently. These approaches are not complete, because they are content-based. Even though they generate important content for the user they do not take into account his preferences. In this research, we investigate the indexing of video content with user-based methods.

On the other hand, researchers have realized that the viewer is not the end of the video production – distribution – consumption chain. Viewer is capable of being a significant node in the chain, playing different roles such as distributor or even producer of the content. In particular, user interactions with the video add value to the content. The cumulative user interactions could be crowdsourced for the benefit of future viewers. For example, some browsing approaches focus on personalization with the user, such as the application framework proposed by Hjelsvolt et al[3] from Siemens, which proposes hotspots and hyperlinks using a personalized model that matches the content against the user profile. Although, this framework is based on users' preferences, it constantly needs their response to various queries in order to build their profile.

According to Money et al (2008) [7], there are two video summarization techniques, internal summarization which analyze internal information from the video stream produced during the production stage of the video lifecycle (such as in [10]) and external summarization techniques which analyze external information during any stage of the video lifecycle (such as in [3],[6]). We propose that the same classification applies to thumbnails generation from videos. SmartSkip[1] is a good example of internal thumbnail generation technique. On the other hand, an external one is proposed on [3].

Moreover, in case of external summarization, two types of information are important [7]. User based information, which is information derived from users' behaviors and interactions with the video, and contextual information, which incorporates information from the environment and not directly from the user. For example, Money et al (2009) [6] propose a video summarization technique that takes into account users' physiological response measures such as heart rate or blood volume to indicate memorable or emotionally engaging video content. On the other hand, Gamhewage et al[9] present a system for video summarization in ubiquitous environment that uses pressure-based floor sensors, a characteristic example of contextual information system. Even though these external summarization techniques take into consideration users' interactions and preferences, they seem to be cumbersome for the users and too complicated to be implemented.

In this paper, we propose an external thumbnail generation method based on user interactions. For this purpose, we have developed a web video player, VideoSkip, which collects interactions of users while they watch the video. Unlike other approaches, not only have the users to response queries during the procedure, but they are not aware of this mining process.

3   VideoSkip Web Video Player

VideoSkip is a web video player we developed to gather interactions of the users while they watch a video. Based on these interactions, representative thumbnails of the video are generated. In fig.1 we can see a screenshot of the player, presenting the main video player window including various buttons and three proposed thumbnail images below.

3.1   Software Tools

In order to implement this web video player, we used a number of software tools such as Google App Engine and YouTube API.

Google App Engine enables building and hosting on the same systems that power Google applications. As a result, users of VideoSkip should have a Google account in order to sign in and watch our videos. Each time a user was logged in the VideoSkip web player, every interaction he had by pressing any button, was recorded and stored in a database provided by Google App Engine for future use (e.g. generating thumbnails).

YouTube API allows developers to use the infrastructure of YouTube and therefore the vast amount of YouTube videos. This API provides us with a chromeless player (a player without controls). We use JavaScript to create our own buttons and implement their functions.

Fig. 1. VideoSkip window with the main video player and three proposed thumbnails below

3.2 Player Buttons

In fig.1 we can see the buttons of VideoSkip player. Rewind button shows the video on the reverse order by jumping three seconds backwards every half a second. The Rewind button changes its label to inform the user about the reverse state of the video player and the user, in order to stop it, has to push again the same button (Stop Rewind) or the Play button. Stop button simply interrupts the playing state of video, returning the player to its initial state of 00:00 sec. Pause button temporarily freeze the video. Play button starts the video. Forward button shows the video on a faster pace. Video player jumps the next three seconds of the video every half a second.

During Rewind and Forward state of the video player, the sound is muted. We decided to use these buttons because they are usually seen in VCR devices and in software playback applications [5] and as a result users should be familiar with them. In our effort to uncover the favorite scenes of the video considering users' preferences, a new button was added, called GoBack. Its main purpose is to replay the last viewed thirty seconds of the video.

Next to the player's button the current time of the video is shown followed by the total time of the video in seconds.

3.3   User Logging

Google App Engine database (the datastore), is used to store users' interactions. Each time a user signs in the web video player application, a new record is created. As it is presented in fig.2, this record includes four fields: a unique id, the username of the user's Google account, the date and a Text variable including all the interactions with the buttons of the web video player.

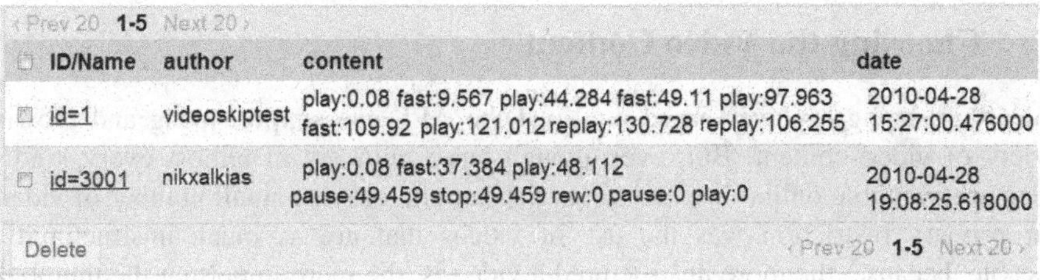

| ‹ Prev 20 **1-5** Next 20 › | | | |
ID/Name	author	content	date
☑ id=1	videoskiptest	play:0.08 fast:9.567 play:44.284 fast:49.11 play:97.963 fast:109.92 play:121.012 replay:130.728 replay:106.255	2010-04-28 15:27:00.476000
☐ id=3001	nikxalkias	play:0.08 fast:37.384 play:48.112 pause:49.459 stop:49.459 rew:0 pause:0 play:0	2010-04-28 19:08:25.618000
Delete		‹ Prev 20 **1-5** Next 20 ›	

Fig. 2. A screenshot of the records' table showing the id, the username (author), the content of the interactions and the date

Whenever a button is pressed, an abbreviation of the button's name and the time it occurred are added to the Text variable. Apparently, the time that is stored is the specific second of the video. The content of the Text variable is used to understand the important segments of the video and therefore generate thumbnails as it is described in the next section.

In order to complete the storing process user must press the Submit and Exit button below the main web video player buttons. When this button is pressed the new record is saved to the datastore, including the exact time of this event. In case of ignoring the Submit and Exit button, the system informs the user with a message box that he has to remain to the web page in order to press that button, before escaping the web video player.

3.4   Thumbnail Generation Algorithm

Every single record is used to generate thumbnails. For each record in the datastore we search for specific button interactions in the content of its Text variable field. Any button or combination could be used.

In our case, taking into account the functionality of GoBack button, we built an algorithm to extract highlight thumbnails. We consider that every video is associated with an array of k cells, where k is the number of the duration of the video in seconds. Initially, the array is empty. Each time user presses the GoBack button the cells' values, matching the last thirty seconds of the video, are incremented by one.

As the number of users who watch the video increases, higher values in specific cells of the array are accumulated. By using a simple sorting technique, the three greatest values of the array are extracted. In order to avoid having consecutive cells as a result, we defined a distance threshold of thirty seconds between them.

The positions of the three greatest values of the array correspond to the time of the most replayed and therefore the most popular video scenes. These three specific scenes are used as proposed thumbnails exactly underneath the web video player.

Whenever a user moves his mouse over a thumbnail, this turns it into a small video player that shows the video from the corresponding time; and in the case of a thumbnail being clicked by the user, the main web video player starts showing the video from the corresponding time respectively.

4   Choosing the Video Content

VideoSkip, being a player based on YouTube API, can support a big and growing variety of video content. But, even though large numbers of almost every kind of video are available online, we had to restrict our choices in a small number of videos. Our primary restriction was the use of videos that are as much unstructured as possible, because, the more unstructured a video is, the more important the thumbnail generation for the future viewers will be. Considering the fact that we use users' interactions to generate thumbnails, another important factor is the attractiveness of a video. In order to have as many users as possible, and therefore maximize the number of interactions, we have to use videos that seem to be important, entertaining and enjoyable in general. Another key factor is the time of a video. In general, YouTube allows video uploading limited to 10 minutes. Although we were able to use videos that exceeded that small limit, we decided not to, because we supposed that it would be tiresome for the majority of users.

In [5], Li et al, in order to test their enhanced browser user interface, used six different types of video, which were classified in three categories: informational audio-centric videos like classroom lectures and conference presentations, informational video-centric like travel and sports videos and narrative-entertainment like television dramas. It was observed that users tent to have content-specific browsing behaviour. In an effort to evaluate our player we included all three categories. In the next chapter we present the usability test of VideoSkip and the interesting results that occurred.

5   Usability Test

Usability is not just the appearance of the user interface. It is related with the way the system reacts with the user and its basic attributes are learnability, efficiency, sufficiency and satisfaction. During the development of any type of project, the steps of usability process should be followed. These steps help user interaction designers to answer crucial questions, during the analysis phase, and supports the design phase. The main tool for this procedure is usability testing that might reveal possible problems[2]. For this purpose there is a variety of tests. A common used usability test that could be applied to VideoSkip is SUS (System Usability Scale) [4].

5.1   Methodology

We decided to select 9 participants (of both genders) as the subjects of our test. The test was conducted within 48 hours online on the internet.

Three videos of different content were shown to users. The first one was a presentation with social meaning «The last lecture» by Randy Pausch representing audio-centric information category, the second one was a sport video «Australia Open 2010 Final Federer vs Murray» which is classified as information video-centric category and the last one which was a segment of a popular comedy TV Series «Big Bang Theory» as a representative of narrative-entertainment video category.

Users were instructed to watch the videos, interact any way they wanted with the player and finally, answer the SUS questionnaire, which was also available online with the help of "Google forms". Users watched the three videos in different order to minimize learning effects. Furthermore, after the completion of this procedure, a friendly conversation took place to discover new users' preferences.

5.2   Usability Testing Results

SUS score was 79.44 which classifies the application in the middle of good and excellent rating. To sum up, this score means that users are able to use VideoSkip easily and successfully. The users, in general, were able to understand directly its components and seemed to be satisfied. All in all, VideoSkip is an acceptable application.

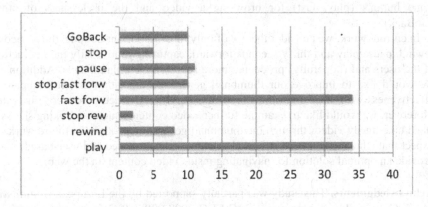

Fig. 3. Button usage during the usability test

According to the users the most interesting of the three videos was «The Last Lecture» by Randy Pausch, although it was the one with the fewer users' interactions. On the other hand, in the sport video «Australia Open 2010 Final Federer vs Murray» the greatest number of interactions was observed, even though users commented that it was an indifferent video. Based on users' interactions, we suppose that the more attractive a video is, the less interactions are taking place due to their attentiveness.

As fig.3 shows, Play and fast forward buttons were the "popular" ones. Considering users' opinion and the study results, we conclude that some buttons are useless. GoBack button seems to be one of them and consequently did not help us to detect favorite scenes of videos.

One major problem is that the use of player requires high speed internet connection. Some participants were annoyed by the delay of video when the player was in forward state. Moreover, one viewer proposed the construction of a multi-sized web video player.

6   Conclusion and Ongoing Research

Even though we did not test VideoSkip with a large number of subjects, we have found some interesting results. We have developed a user-based video indexing system and we have produced initial evidence that users' interactions with a web video player could play an important role towards enhancing the browsing experience by generating thumbnails. As long as the community of users watching videos online is growing, more and more interactions are going to be gathered and therefore, automatically generated thumbnails would represent effectively the most important scenes of the videos. We also expect that the combination of richer user profiles and content metadata might provide opportunities for additional personalization of the thumbnails.

Based on our hypothesis, we identified the relation between the content of the video and the reactions that occurred. Moreover, we understood the importance of some buttons (play, fast) for browsing a video and the uselessness of others (GoBack).

In current work, we consider the use of only three important buttons: thirty seconds rewind, pause/play and thirty seconds forward, capturing more easily the interactions of the users and (hopefully) producing more representative thumbnails. Additionally, we would like to improve our thumbnail generation algorithm and to compare its effectiveness with other algorithms or with experts' (e.g. video producers') indexing. Moreover, we would like to examine further video contents such as cooking shows or stand up comedy videos through the thumbnail generation process. In future work, we expect that a balanced mix of hybrid algorithms (content-based and user-based) might provide an optimal solution for navigating inside video content on the web.

Acknowledgments. This study was partially supported by the European Commission Marie Curie Fellowship program (MC-ERG-2008-230894). We are also grateful to the participants of the study and to many constructive comments by the anonymous reviewers.

References

1. Drucker, S.M., Glatzer, A., Mar, S.D., Wong, C.: SmartSkip: Consumer level browsing and skipping of digital video content. In: Proceedings of the SIGCHI Conference on Human Factors in Computing Systems, pp. 219–226. ACM Press, New York (2002), http://doi.acm.org/10.1145/503376.503416
2. Ferre, X., Juristo, N., Windl, H., Constantine, L.: Usability Basics for Software Developers. IEEE Software 18(1), 22–29 (2001), doi:http://dx.doi.org/10.1109/52.903160
3. Hjelsvold, R., Vdaygiri, S., Leaute, Y.: Web-based personalization and management of interactive video. In: Proceedings of the 10th International Conference on World Wide Web, pp. 129–139. ACM Press, New York (2001), doi:http://doi.acm.org/10.1145/371920.371969
4. Holyer, A.: Methods For Evaluating User Interfaces 1993. Cognitive Science Research Paper No. 301, School of Cognitive and Computing Sciences. University of Sussex, UK (1993)
5. Li, F.C., Gupta, A., Sanocki, E., He, L., Rui, Y.: Browsing digital video. In: Proceedings of the SIGCHI Conferenece on Human Factors in Computing Systems, CHI 2000, Hague, The Netherlands, April 01-06, pp. 169–176. ACM Press, New York (2000), http://doi.acm.org/10.1145/332040.332425
6. Money, A.G., Agius, H.: Analysing user physiological responses for affective video summarization. Displays 30(2), 59–70 (2009), doi:http://dx.doi.org/10.1016/j.displa.2008.12.003
7. Money, A.G., Agius, H.: Video summarization: A conceptual framework and survey of the state of the art. Journal of Visual Communication and Image Representation 19(2), 121–143 (2008), doi:http://dx.doi.org/10.1016/j.jvcir.2007.04.002
8. Shamma, D.A., Shaw, R., Shafton, P.L., Liu, Y.: Watch What I Watch: using community activity to understand content. In: Proceedings of the International Workshop on Multimedia Information Retrieval, MIR 2007, pp. 275–284. ACM Press (2007), doi:http://doi.acm.org/10.1145/1290082.1290120
9. Silva, G.C., Yamasaki, T., Aizawa, K.: Evaluation of video summarization for large number of cameras in ubiquitous home. In: Proceedings of the 13th Annual ACM International Conference on Multimedia, pp. 820–828. ACM Press, New York (2005), doi:http://doi.acm.org/10.1145/1101149.1101329
10. Takahashi, Y., Nitta, N., Babaguchi, N.: Video summarization for large sports video archives. In: Proceedings of the International Conference on Multimedia and Expo (ICME), pp. 1170–1173 (2005)

Metadata-Based Content Management and Sharing System for Improved User Experience

Markus Waltl, Christian Raffelsberger, Christian Timmerer,
and Hermann Hellwagner

Klagenfurt University, Inst. of Information Technology, Multimedia Communication Group
Universitätsstraße 65-67, 9020 Klagenfurt, Austria
{firstname.lastname}@itec.uni-klu.ac.at

Abstract. In the past years the amount of multimedia content on the Internet or in home networks has been drastically increasing. Instead of buying traditional media (such as CDs or DVDs) users tend to buy online media. This leads to the difficulty of managing the content (e.g., movies, images). A vast amount of tools for content management exists but they are mainly focusing on one type of content (e.g., only images). Furthermore, most of the available tools are not configurable to the user's preferences and cannot be accessed by different devices (e.g., TV, computer, mobile phone) in the home network. In this paper we present a UPnP A/V-based system for managing and sharing audio/visual content in home environments which is configurable to the user's preferences. Furthermore, the paper depicts how this system can be used to improve the user experience by using MPEG-V.

Keywords: Metadata, UPnP A/V, Content Management, Content Sharing, MPEG-V, Sensory Effects, User Experience.

1 Introduction

The amount of content, i.e., movies, images, and music, has drastically increased in the last years [1]. As a consequence, users have increasing difficulties in managing their content and finding a specific movie or image. There are different techniques (e.g., searching, browsing) to reduce the amount of data a user has to look through before finding the desired content. The major problem with the default techniques is that they are not configurable to the user's preferences and to the content itself.

The issue of not being able to configure the search/browse engine to the user's preference is addressed by the metadata-based *Content Management and Sharing System* (CMSS) presented in this paper. The CMSS provides the ability to browse content in a configurable tree instead of searching for content. This approach provides the user the functionality to browse for a specific content (e.g., movies from the action genre released during the 1980s). Furthermore, the browsing tree provided by the CMSS can be dynamically changed through a user-editable configuration. This allows the user to adjust the system to her/his preferences. Furthermore, the configuration can support all kinds of content, e.g., music, images, videos, or MPEG-V metadata.

F. Alvarez and C. Costa (Eds.): UCMEDIA 2010, LNICST 60, pp. 132–140, 2012.

The support of all kinds of content allows for a wide range of possible usage scenarios, e.g., for increasing the user experience during consumption of multimedia content. Moreover, the CMSS allows editing of metadata (e.g., author, title) that belongs to specific content and provides content via UPnP A/V [2] and RTP/RTSP [3,4]. The content offered by the CMSS can be consumed by a large number of devices without special requirements (e.g., a set-top box) because of the usage of the UPnP A/V standard.

The remainder of this paper is organized as follows. Section 2 describes the architecture of the CMSS which has been developed during the course of the INTERMEDIA project. Section 3 provides an overview of MPEG-V Media Context and Control which is a standard under development for enhancing the user experience. Section 4 presents how to combine it with the CMSS. Conclusions and future work items are presented in Section 5.

2   Architecture of the Content Management and Sharing System

Fig. 1 depicts the architecture of the CMSS. Most of the CMSS is based on Java for providing portability to various systems, only some external libraries are not written in Java (e.g., native extraction libraries). The CMSS consists of components for managing, storing, importing and streaming multimedia content. The system is a Web application running on a JBoss Application Server [5] and uses MySQL [6] as metadata storage. However, the CMSS comprises two different types of storages: one for storing metadata using MySQL and one for storing the actual media content utilizing the file system. The CMSS provides a Web interface to enable a user to upload new content to the system or to modify existing metadata. On the other side of the chain, the user can browse this content via UPnP A/V [2] which is a well established standard supported by many multimedia devices and applications. UPnP A/V provides services for retrieving a list of the available contents and for requesting a specific content. The user at the consumer side can use UPnP A/V for retrieving the desired content which will be transferred via HTTP to the MediaRenderer or streamed via RTP/RTSP [3,4] to a media player. When using RTP/RTSP, the user has a control mechanism over the data stream of the content. She/he can play, pause, rewind, or fast forward the content without downloading the whole content like in HTTP. The RTP/RTSP support is provided by the *VideoLan Manager* (VLM) that is a component of the *VideoLan Player* (VLC) [7]. For providing UPnP A/V within the CMSS, the *Cyberlink for Java* [8] library is used. To be compatible with UPnP A/V, software applications or hardware devices have to include at least one UPnP A/V device (MediaServer, ControlPoint or MediaRenderer) and its mandatory services. The CMSS includes a UPnP A/V MediaServer. There are applications providing several devices, thus, the logical separation may not be found in practice (e.g., a TV that implements both ControlPoint and MediaRenderer).

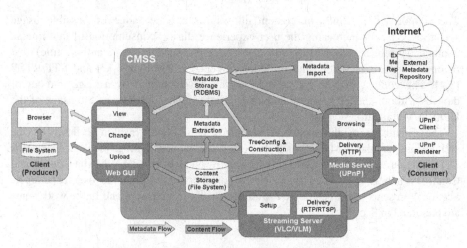

Fig. 1. Architecture of the Content Management and Sharing System

The CMSS offers various tools that reduce the effort for the user to add metadata to newly uploaded content. For example, low-level metadata (i.e., bit rate, codec, resolution, etc.) is automatically extracted by an extraction chain consisting of *Mime-util* [9], *Libextractor* [10] and *FFmpeg* [11]. These tools can be replaced or extended with additional extractors. The resulting low-level metadata information is stored within the metadata storage for later retrieval. The content itself is placed in the content storage.

After uploading, the user has the possibility to add high-level metadata (i.e., cast, director, artist, plot, etc.). This can happen manually or via metadata importers. Currently, two importers are available: for videos, from the TheMovieDB.org [12] repository and, for music, from the MusicBrainz [13] repository. The CMSS supports adding new importers as well as modifying and removing the existing importers.

A problem which conflicts with the user-centric approach is the pre-defined (static) structure of the content list in many UPnP A/V MediaServers. Therefore, the CMSS allows the user to customize the view (i.e., presented tree structure) on the metadata via the Web interface. The configuration of the view is stored in a text file which allows the user to customize the tree structure in an easy way. We selected a simple text based structure instead of other more complex representation forms (e.g., XML) because it is easy to learn, read and modify. Note that the system can be modified to allow other configuration representations. The configuration consists of one or more configuration lines, where each configuration line consists of one or more keywords. These keywords are mapped to certain metadata tags that are included in the database (e.g., title, genre, resolution, language). Additionally, two special keywords (*Static* and *Alphabet*) are defined. The *Static* keyword is used for providing a label which can be used for renaming or restructuring the content tree. The *Alphabet* keyword can be used to further improve the structure by automatically grouping a long list of nodes (e.g., performers, titles) based on their initial character. We limited the *Alphabet* keyword to only support a subset of the available database fields because it is not very useful to define *Alphabet* for various fields (e.g., numerical fields such as bit rate, resolution, duration). Each line in the configuration file denotes a branch in the tree. To build a hierarchy of nodes, multiple nodes can be linked with the "->" operator. The node at the left side of the operator is the parent, the right one is the child. Equal, or partially equal, branches are automatically merged.

This functionality is an approach to provide a user-centric content presentation which allows the user to personalize the view on the content. For example, if the user only wants to have images and music, she/he can remove the entries for videos from the configuration.

An example for a small CMSS tree configuration is shown in Listing 1 and an abstract representation of the resulting tree is depicted in Listing 2. The example presents a tree which consists of a static label *Genres* that is defined by *Static:Genres*. The next keyword *Genre* specifies to query all genres that exist in the database and to insert them into the tree. Every genre is further divided into two separate branches: *Performers* and *Decades*. The *Performers* label consists of a list of the names of the performers within this specific genre. The second line of the configuration includes a *Decades* label which introduces a list of decades that are based on the release date of the content. For example, a historical movie released in the year 1965 will be listed under the decade "1960s" which is located in the "History" branch.

Listing 1. Example CMSS tree configuration

```
Static:Genres->Genre->Static:Performers->Performer
Static:Genres->Genre->Static:Decades->Decade
```

Listing 2. Abstract representation of the example tree

```
Genres
  |-> Action
  |-> Horror
    |-> Decades
      |-> 1970s
      |-> . . .
    |-> Performers
      |-> Christopher Lee
      |-> . . .
  |-> . . .
```

Note that this example tree currently only comprises movies but can consist of all types of content. Furthermore, the presented configuration file of the CMSS allows, in contrast to other systems, an on-the-fly modification of the content view and could be extended in the future to provide every user a different view on the content.

During the development of the CMSS, an extension to UPnP A/V DIDL-Lite [14] was introduced. We call this extension *bundling*. The bundling feature allows the user to associate several content and metadata files for combined usage. Thus, additional information can be delivered along with the content. With this method it is possible to send external metadata files, such as subtitles, MPEG-V sensory effects, karaoke lyrics, etc. to enhance the user experience while consuming multimedia content. Bundling information is stored within the desc element that is already defined in DIDL-Lite. Note that the desc element requires a namespace that defers from the DIDL-Lite namespace for all child elements. Therefore, we redefined the existing res element within a new namespace. These elements contain all information that is needed to retrieve a bundled item. For example, if a movie contains only an English subtitle but the user wants to have other subtitles she/he could bundle them to the movie (e.g., German or French subtitles) which are available as separate files. An example of such a DIDL-Lite description can be found in Listing 3. The example shows a video item that comprises information about title, artists, genres and director. Furthermore, the DIDL-Lite includes information about the location of the video. In this example, the video is available for HTTP download and as an RTP/RTSP stream. The description element announces a bundled item. Here, the bundled item represents a French subtitle file for that video.

Listing 3. Example DIDL-Lite description with bundled content

```
<DIDL-Lite>
 <item id="3" parentID="-32232" restricted="1">
  <upnp:class>object.item.videoItem</upnp:class>
  <dc:title>Babylon A.D.</dc:title>
  <upnp:artist>G. Depardieu, V. Diesel</upnp:artist>
  <upnp:genre>Thriller, Action, Sci-Fi</upnp:genre>
  <upnp:director>Mathieu Kassovitz</upnp:director>
  <res protocolInfo="http-get:*:video/mpeg:*" nrAudioChannels="5">
   http://<ip>:<port>/Export?id=3&amp;file=BabylonAD.avi</res>
  <res protocolInfo="rtsp-rtp-udp:*:video/mpeg:*"
   nrAudioChannels="5">rtsp://<ip>:<port>/vid3.avi</res>
  <desc nameSpace="urn:schemas-uniklu:09-2009:intermedia" id="3">
   <didl-ext:bundle>
    <didl-ext:res protocolInfo="http-get:*:text/plain:*">
     http://<ip>:<port>/Export?id=29&amp;file=BabylonAD_French.srt
    </didl-ext:res>
   </didl-ext:bundle>
  </desc>
 </item>
</DIDL-Lite>
```

Basically, container formats provide a very similar functionality as bundling. However, there are two main reasons why we introduced bundling instead of using existing container formats (e.g., MP4). First, a multimedia player has to be able to support the container format in order to be able to obtain the contained metadata or additional resources. Second, the whole file including all resources and metadata has to be stored and delivered to the user. There is no way to select only the desired parts of the package.

As the CMSS uses UPnP A/V to share its data with other devices, bundling should be compatible with this technology. Bundling information has to be propagated within the UPnP A/V network without breaking the compatibility with standard UPnP A/V actions. Players which do not support bundling only retrieve the main content (e.g., the video) and ignore additional information advertised in further items. Players supporting bundling can download and use the additional information, e.g., the additional French subtitles, as shown in Listing 3.

By using the bundling approach the user can freely decide what she/he wants to consume and does not have to download unwanted or unnecessary information. This reduces the needed bandwidth and storage space at the client.

3   MPEG-V Media Context and Control

MPEG-V Media Context and Control is an ISO/IEC standard under development. It will allow the integration of virtual worlds into the real world (e.g., via augmented reality) and vice versa (e.g., via avatars). For example, with appropriate devices (e.g., fans, vibration chairs, lamps) a movie can be enriched with additional effects (e.g., wind, vibration, light) for enhancing the user experience. The additional effects are described and stored in so-called *Sensory Effect Metadata* (SEM) descriptions. These descriptions are defined in Part 3 of MPEG-V [15].

The SEM description is shipped with the content (e.g., movie, audio, image) or can be downloaded from a remote storage (e.g., the Internet). Both, the SEM description and the content are delivered to MPEG-V-capable devices for playback. Fig. 2 depicts the concept of such sensory effects.

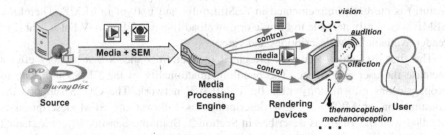

Fig. 2. The Concept of Sensory Effects [18]

Initial user studies [16,17] were conducted in the area of sensory effects for videos and yielded promising results. These results show that sensory effects are most likely to enhance the experience of users watching movies accompanied by a SEM description.

The first user study [16] presents the benefits of using sensory effects along with multimedia content. Here the participants were asked to rate the enhancement of a video with sensory effects with respect to the same video sequence without sensory effects. The results shown in [16] indicate that for different genres sensory effects are perceived differently. For example, sensory effects lead to a worthwhile user experience for action movies and documentaries while being less informative for news.

The second user study [17] presents the utility of sensory effects which means how sensory effects improve the perceived video quality. In this study two video sequences were shown with various bit rates. The videos were presented twice to the participants, one time without sensory effects and another time with sensory effects. The participants had to rate the video quality of the test sequences. The results show an improvement of the perceived video quality by using sensory effects. On average, the result for a sequence accompanied by sensory effects is 0.5 mean opinion score (MOS) higher than for the same sequence without sensory effects. More detailed results can be found in [17].

4   Usage of MPEG-V Context and Control with the CMSS

The test-bed introduced in [18] is able to work with the CMSS. The *Sensory Effect Video Annotation Tool* (SEVino) can be used for generating SEM descriptions for a video. The *Sensory Effect Simulator* (SESim) is a simulator for SEM descriptions and does not provide real-world stimulation (e.g., real wind or vibration effects). For providing real-world stimulation the *Sensory Effect Media Player* (SEMP) [16] was developed which renders sensory effects on the amBX system [19].

These tools and the CMSS are combined in the following way: on the provider side of the CMSS, SEVino allows a user to generate SEM descriptions for a video and upload the video and the SEM description to the CMSS. On the consumer side, SESim and SEMP can be used for simulating and rendering, respectively, the effects that are contained in the SEM description. UPnP A/V support (including the bundling feature) is currently implemented in SESim only, and not yet in SEMP. Therefore, SEMP is currently not able to browse or download files via UPnP A/V but it is able to render available SEM descriptions and videos.

The first user study that was presented in Section 3 shows that sensory effects increase the user experience. The bundling functionality of the CMSS is a way to propagate this information within the UPnP A/V network. The CMSS supports the consumption of MPEG-V SEM descriptions as follows: the SEM description is bundled with the video, as described in Section 2. Both, the Sensory Effect Metadata and the video are still stored separately in the CMSS but the user has only to browse one of the two files (e.g., only the video). Information about the bundled file is advertised in the DIDL-Lite description and can be used to download both files at the same time.

The second user study in Section 3 concludes that the perceived video quality can be increased by using sensory effects. Therefore, the storage requirements of the CMSS can be reduced by decreasing the bit rate of the video and instead supplying sensory effects. As a result, the network load and bandwidth requirements for retrieving the content from the CMSS are also reduced. Results showed that the video sequence *Earth* with a bit rate of 2204 kb/s and accompanied by a SEM description was perceived as being better than the same video sequence with a bit rate of

6701 kb/s without a SEM description. The used SEM description had a file size of approximately 3 Kbytes. Hence, the bit rate can be reduced by approximately 66% by using Sensory Effects, without decreasing the perceived video quality.

Note that there is a large variation in bit rates and perceived quality for other video sequences. Furthermore, for other video sequences the reduction can be much less than for this example but can still be feasible. For more detailed results refer to [17].

5   Conclusion and Future Work

In this paper we presented a metadata-based content management and sharing system which allows modifications, extensions and replacements in various parts of the system. Furthermore, the paper described a user-centric configuration that enables the user to create an individual configuration for displaying her/his content. Further, we introduced an extension of UPnP A/V for bundling content. This feature is an alternative to container formats and can be used to associate metadata or multimedia content which are stored in separate files. Moreover, the paper presented MPEG-V and how the CMSS can deliver bundled SEM descriptions within a UPnP A/V network in order to enrich the user experience. Finally, the CMSS is one of the first applications that support the enrichment of video content by providing bundled SEM descriptions via UPnP A/V.

Future work items are the integration of an adaptation and transcoding unit for providing the most suitable format (e.g., in terms of quality, resolution, bit rate) for various devices. Furthermore, UPnP A/V does not support user profiles which enable every user to have her/his own view on the content and preferences. A possible solution for this problem would be to integrate UPnP-UP (UPnP User Profile) as described in [20]. Another future work item would be the evaluation of the current system, for example, an evaluation on the question: "Is it faster and easier to find a specific content item via customized browsing than via searching?" Additionally, SEMP will be extended to support the retrieval of videos and SEM descriptions via UPnP A/V.

Acknowledgments. This work was supported in part by the EC in the context of the NoE INTERMEDIA (NoE 038419).

References

1. Gantz, J.F., et al.: The Expanding Digital Universe: A Forecast of Worldwide Information Growth Through 2010. IDC White Paper (2007)
2. UPnP Forum: MediaServer V 1.0 and MediaRenderer V 1.0,
   http://upnp.org/standardizeddcps/mediaserver.asp
3. Schulzrinne, H., Casner, S., Frederick, R., Jacobson, V.: RTP: A Transport Protocol for Real-Time Applications. RFC 3550. Internet Engineering Task Force (2003),
   http://www.ietf.org/rfc/rfc3550.txt

4. Schulzrinne, H., Rao, A., Lanphier, R.: Real Time Streaming Protocol (RTSP). RFC 2326. Internet Engineering Task Force (1998), http://www.ietf.org/rfc/rfc2326.txt
5. JBoss Application Server, http://www.jboss.org
6. MySQL, http://www.mysql.com/
7. VideoLan, http://www.videolan.org
8. CyberGarage: CyberLink for Java, http://www.cybergarage.org/cgi-bin/twiki/view/Main/CyberLinkForJava
9. Mime-util (Mime Type Detection Utility), http://sourceforge.net/projects/mime-util/
10. GNU Libextractor, http://gnunet.org/libextractor/
11. FFmpeg, http://ffmpeg.org/
12. TheMovieDB.org, http://www.themoviedb.org/
13. MusicBrainz, http://musicbrainz.org/
14. Debique, K., Igarashi, T., Kou, S., Moonen, J., Ritchie, J., Schults, G., Walker, M.: ContentDirectory:1 Service Template Version 1.01 (2002), http://www.upnp.org/standardizeddcps/documents/ContentDirectory1.0.pdf
15. ISO/IEC 23005-3 FCD: Information technology – Media context and control – Sensory information. ISO/IEC JTC 1/SC 29/WG 11/N10987, Xi'an, China (2009)
16. Waltl, M., Timmerer, C., Hellwagner, H.: Increasing the User Experience of Multimedia Presentations with Sensory Effects. In: 11th Int'l. Workshop on Image Analysis for Multimedia Interactive Services (WIAMIS 2010), Desenzano del Garda, Italy (2010)
17. Waltl, M., Timmerer, C., Hellwagner, H.: Improving the Quality of Multimedia Experience through Sensory Effects. In: 2nd Int'l. Workshop on Quality of Multimedia Experience (QoMEX 2010), Trondheim, Norway (2010)
18. Waltl, M., Timmerer, C., Hellwagner, H.: A Test-Bed for Quality of Multimedia Experience Evaluation of Sensory Effects. In: 1st Int'l. Workshop on Quality of Multimedia Experience (QoMEX 2009), San Diego, USA (2009)
19. amBX UK Ltd., http://www.ambx.com
20. Sales, T.B.M.d., Sales, L.M.d., Pereira, M., Almeida, H., Perkusich, A., Gorgônio, K., Sales Jr., M.A.d.: Towards the UPnP-UP: Enabling User Profile to Support Customized Services in UPnP Networks. In: 2nd Int'l. Conference on Mobile Ubiquitous Computing, Systems, Services and Technologies (UBICOMM 2008), Washington DC, USA (2008)

An Application Framework for Seamless Synchronous Collaboration Support in Ubiquitous Computing Environments

Seunghyun Han, Niels A. Nijdam, and Nadia Magnenat-Thalmann

MIRALab, University of Geneva, 7, rte de Drize, 1227, Geneva, Switzerland
{han,nijdam,thalmann}@miralab.ch

Abstract. Dynamic and heterogeneous nature of ubiquitous computing environments introduces additional requirements to support synchronous collaboration. Such requirements include support of various interaction types, flexible data couplings, and transparent context adaptation. To meet those requirements, in this paper, we propose the manipulation based application model. In comparison to the presentation semantics split model [5], we introduce the manipulation in between the presentation and shared semantics. A manipulation is a fragment of the semantics, which is dynamically created when a presentation requires personalized interaction to the shared semantics. A manipulation enables transparent context adaptation by migrating its states to a new manipulation of the different presentation to adapt the current context, e.g., user location change. We prototyped the proposed application framework and tested the feasibility of the framework.

Keywords: Synchronous collaboration, ubiquitous computing, application framework, context adaptation.

1 Introduction

With the proliferation of networks and computers, the vision of ubiquitous computing [1][10] is realized in everyday living environments such as a home and an office where is often populated by multiple users simultaneously. Within such an environment, collaboration among a group of users is conducted to accomplish a common task, exploiting a wide range of devices in many different shapes, sizes and computing capabilities while moving around in the environment. There have been several research efforts [2][6] on nomadic users to collaborate with each other. They assume that each participant uses a dedicated device with similar capabilities, e.g., mobile phone, PDA, notebook, and user mobility is handled at the network level e.g., handoff management [8]. However, this does not hold for ubiquitous computing environments anymore. It means that, while participating in collaboration, each participant does not need to stick to one device and can change their devices for better utilization of available devices. For instance, a user prefers to conduct a video conferencing with a large wall-display rather than a small display on PDA as he enters to his living room from outside, adapting to dynamic context changes [3].

F. Alvarez and C. Costa (Eds.): UCMEDIA 2010, LNICST 60, pp. 141–149, 2012.
© Institute for Computer Sciences, Social Informatics and Telecommunications Engineering 2012

To successfully support such dynamic adaptation, Computer Supported Collaborative Work (CSCW) technologies are faced with a new challenge: to support dynamic changes of interaction devices without losing the consistency of shared information in the presence of context changes. To meet the new requirement, in this paper, a new application model extending the presentation and semantic split model is proposed. In this model, a collaborative application is separated into five parts: semantics, presentation, manipulation, context adaptation, and session control. The semantics represents the shared data in a collaborative application. The presentation acts as a function for the interactive control between users and the shared semantics. It transforms the shared states into a form that is perceivable by a user. The manipulation provides methods to process shared semantics. Multiple different manipulations can be dynamically coupled to a subset of the shared data in the semantics, so that the data in the shared semantics can be processed in different ways by the coupled manipulations. The main role of the manipulation is to maintain the consistency between the shared semantics during any changes of presentations while adapting to the transition of devices. Two types of sessions are defined, a user session and collaboration session. A user session is defined as 'a group of application components, devices on which application components are resided and their bindings which are used by a user within a given time'. A collaboration session is composed of a set of user sessions in the current environment. The context adaptation triggers changes of a user session based on current context. Context adaptation is different 'user by user' as well as 'environment by environment'. We prototyped the proposed application framework with the runtime support and built several applications based on the framework.

The remainder of this paper is organized as follows. In section 2, we describe the requirements for multi-user collaboration in ubiquitous computing environments. In section 3, we describe the proposed application model. Section 4 describes the implementation of our prototype system and its applications respectively. Conclusion is followed in section 5.

2   Requirement Analysis

One of the key characteristics of ubiquitous computing environments is the dynamic change of context of users and environments. This introduces two key technical requirements to support seamless collaboration among users in ubiquitous computing environments. First, users are not just limited to utilize one dedicated device, e.g., mobile phone, PDA, and notebook, but have more freedom to exploit diverse and different set of devices while participating in a collaborative session. It requires a polymorphic presentation adaptation to overcome the resource heterogeneity of the client devices while providing suitable responsiveness to users. This means that the presentation to a user, which includes view and interface, i.e., frame size, frame rate and user interfaces, has to be dynamically adapted to the current device context such as processing power, memory size, display size, and network condition at runtime. Secondly context changes cannot be fully predefined at the application design stage, because the context can be different for each user, as well as from one environment to another. It requires the ability to embracing the context changes but still clearly separate the context adaptation from the application semantics. The context adaptation must be transparent to the target user as well to all other participants.

3   The Proposed Approach

A collaborative application is a mean by which users are able to perform a common collaborative task. The proposed model is specifically designed for building collaborative applications; with the goal that it provides application-developers with a suitable abstraction that overcomes the heterogeneity of devices and diversity of contexts in ubiquitous computing environments.

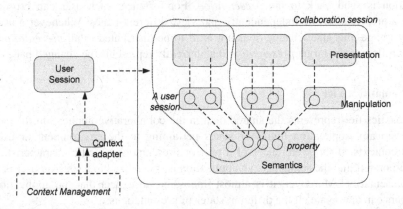

Fig. 1. The proposed application model. It is composed of the five elements: semantics, presentation, manipulation, context adapter, and session.

The proposed application model defines five elements: semantics, manipulation, presentation, session, and context adapter as shown Fig. 1. The semantics, manipulation, and presentation are the application base-level building blocks and are strictly related to the application domain functionality. The session manages the composition of the three base-level components and implements the application meta-level. It stores information about the user session in the current environment. A context adapter monitors any context changes in the environment and changes session composition accordingly.

3.1   Presentation Tier

In ubiquitous computing environments, we cannot simply assume that users share the exactly same view of the shared data for collaboration due to the following reasons. First, devices have different capabilities in terms of display and processing resources in an environment. Secondly, the available devices can be changed due to context changes. Last, users can exploit a diversity of devices to participate into collaboration based on the users' preferences. We handle the situations in presentation tier. The presentation tier can be seen as a bag of *presentations*. It maintains a set of *presentations* and is responsible for accessing and manipulating the *semantics* through corresponding *manipulation*. Each user has its own presentation tier; within this tier each *presentation* is specific to one device. A *presentation* acts as a function of an interactive control between users and functionality which transforms application data in the shared *semantics* into a perceivable form. This implies that each *presentation* should be developed specifically to fit a device, because each device has different capabilities (e.g. display and processing capacity). The *presentation* receives user-actions as events and responds to these 'actions'. Multiple different *presentations* are selectively coupled with specific data within the shared *semantics* through *manipulation*. Each *presentation* selectively registers its interests to a specific *manipulation*. Whenever a specific state of the shared *semantics* is changed a notification is send back to the *presentation*. For instance, each user can browse through a presentation file independently and view different pages. Whenever a user changes a page, this state change does not need to be distributed to all *presentations* but only reflect to the target *presentation* that currently represents the changed page.

3.2 Semantics Tier

The semantics tier represents the shared data in the collaborative application. It does not contain any application logics or states pertaining to the environment or user specific contexts. If the preferences of a user or presentation-specific characteristics are incorporated into the semantics, an application is specialized to a specific user or a target presentation. Moreover, it is almost impossible to expect that the application developers can anticipate all the different states of presentations.

Unlike the model in distributed MVC model [6][7][9], we explicitly decouple manipulation functionality from the shared data. This allows users to share only data with different functionality and representations, so called 'polymorphic collaboration'. The semantics is responsible for notifying any states changes in the shared data. It can support various forms of interactions by dynamically binding different types of manipulations to the shared semantic. It persistently keeps its states, which allows users to continue a collaborative task by reincarnating the shared *semantics* when users re-initiate the collaborative task.

3.3 Manipulation Tier

The manipulation tier maintains a set of manipulations and is responsible for linking *presentations* and *semantics*. A *manipulation* specifies how the shared *semantics* is manipulated by *presentations*. We define a *manipulation* as follows. Let q be a semantic and p be a manipulation for q. p provides functions for manipulating q. p can have additional attributes and methods. Correspondence between p and q is represented by its *link*, which enables update propagation between p and q. A *link* between p and q could be dynamically mapped if necessary.

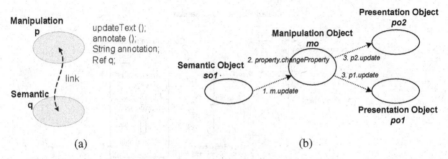

Fig. 2. (a) represents a relationship between semantics and manipulation. (b) represents m:1 relationship between manipulation and two presentations.

Fig. 2(a) shows an example of the relationship between a *manipulation* and a *semantics*. A *semantics q* provides presentation material *q.material* as a shared data. A *manipulation p* can have reference of *q* as its *link*. It provides *p.updateText* method to change *q.material*. A *manipulation p* also defines additional property *p.annotation* and additional method *p.annotate* for personal manipulation. Each *manipulation* can provide different functionality of a shared *semantics*. It implies that multiple different *manipulations* are bound to a shared *semantics* so that the shared *semantics* can be manipulated in different ways. The *manipulation* support m:1 relationship (more than one presentation per manipulation) as shown in Fig. 2(b). It is useful when multiple devices for a user share the same functionality of a collaborative application. For example, in case of presentation manager application, a user can review the same slide with a desktop display (*po1*) and a wall-display (*po2*) in his room while other users are collaborating in their own rooms (different environment). A personal annotation made by a user (*mo*) cannot be distributed other participants and it also does not change the shared data (*so1*). In this case, the manipulation notification should not be distributed to other participants, thus reducing the number of interaction events.

3.4   Context Adaptation Tier

Collaborative applications in ubiquitous computing environments are influenced by external changes that affect the composition of the collaborative application at runtime, and therefore collaborative applications require support in order to adapt to these context changes dynamically. It usually alters the application composition according to the current context of the users and environment.

Figure 3 outlines the basic flow of a context adaptation process as an example of location context adapter. Each time a user moves from one place to another, the context manager invokes the notify method of the registered location context adapter. The location adapter obtains a list of available devices from presence manager in the execution infrastructure. Next, it uses the interfaces of the target user's session, in order to change between devices and to migrate states. This is specific to the target environment and may not be used to another environment. A context adapter also can change a specific property of *manipulation*, *presentation*, and *semantics* using the target user's session, if the developer knows specific properties of them.

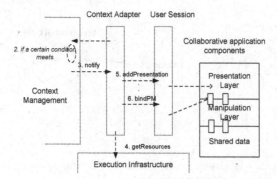

Fig. 3. Dynamic context adaptation process

3.5   Collaboration Session Control Tier

We define two types of sessions, a user session and collaboration session. A user session is defined as 'a group of application components and devices on which the application components are resided, and their bindings that are used by a user within a given time'. Collaboration session is composed of a set of user sessions in the current environment. Collaborative session control such as dynamic user join and leave is managed by collaborative session control and context adaptation is control by a user session.

A user session maintains meta-level information of currently exploiting devices and software components of a user. It is dynamically changed at runtime when a target user changes devices or application components adapting to a context change. It also persistently preserves the session states such as device ID and references of software components when a user leaves the current collaboration session. This persistently preserved session states are reused when the user re-joins to the collaborative session. It reduces user's distractions to manually reconfigure the application components.

4   Implementation

Fig. 4 shows the overall architectures of the runtime environment of the proposed framework.

The session description is environment independent so that it lists the components of a session and their requirements. It contains a list of entries that describe each required component. Each entry contains name-value pairs to specify the component name and type, and the resources required by the component. When users create a collaborative session or a new user joins the session, a list of matching resources are obtained by system services. Context adaptation is user specific so that the each user session manages its own context adapters. The context adaptation logic is different from one environment to another so that the context adaptation types are provided with a separate description. A Collaboration Session Manager (CSM) is generic to all kinds of collaborative applications and only one exists in an environment. It is a kind of abstract application factory. It receives an abstract session description. It interacts with system services to create environment specific applications. Its key roles are to create application component instances, bind them together, and pass the result, which contain meta-information of the user session, to the Session Manager. A Node Manager mirrors the CSM, but is limited to only one node. When a device is entered into an environment the Node Manager is registered to Presence Manager so that the device participates in the environment. It is a daemon-like process that is always running on each individual node and responsible for spawning an Object Reconfiguration Manager (ORM). It creates an ORM whenever lifecycle management requests are invoked. It also instantiates the Migration Manager when migration of an application object which currently runs on the node is requested. The Object Reconfiguration Manager is responsible for managing the lifecycle of objects, which includes create, destroy, suspend, resume, save and restore states of objects. To create a presentation object, it first checks if the target object is preserved in the State Repository. If it exists, it restores the object; otherwise, it creates a new presentation object and its corresponding manipulation objects by downloading executables of the target object. Then, it registers presentation and manipulation objects to the Node Manager.

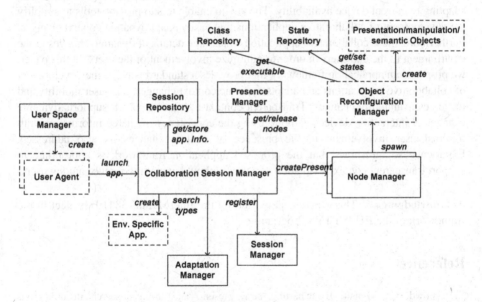

Fig. 4. Runtime support of the proposed application framework

We built a collaborative telemedicine system for real-time and interactive segmentation of volumetric medical images [4] based on the proposed application framework. In this application, users can utilize diverse devices, i.e., mobile phone, UMPC, notebook, interactive table, to collaborate with each other as shown in Fig. 5. Users can also seamlessly collaborate with each other while moving from one place to another with minimal distractions from the computing devices.

Fig. 5. Collaborative telemedicine system built based on the proposed application framework

5   Conclusion

One of key differences of synchronous collaboration in ubiquitous computing environments from mobile computing is that users can dynamically change their devices adapting to current device availability. The key to enable it is to provide tools to simplify the development of collaborative applications that easily adapt dynamic context changes. Furthermore, these collaborative applications must hide details of dynamic changes in the environment to the end users in order to minimize involvement of the users. In this paper, we proposed an application framework that provides a standard way for the development of collaborative applications and adapts dynamic context changes, e.g., user mobility and resources availability changes. Transparent context adaptation, which supports dynamic changes of interaction devices without losing the consistency of shared information with minimal user involvement in the presence of context changes, is also addressed. Experience so far shows that the proposed application framework is appropriate to support transparent context adaptation of a user without having interference among users.

Acknowledgments. This work is supported by the InterMedia (38419) project in the framework of the EU IST FP6 Programme.

References

1. Abowd, G., Mynatt, E.: Charting past, present, and future research in ubiquitous computing. ACM Transactions on Computer-Human Interaction 7(1), 29–58 (2000)
2. Cheng, S., Huang, A., Garlan, D., Schmerl, B., Steenkiste, P.: Rainbow: Architecture-Based Self Adaptation with Reusable Infrastructure. IEEE Computer 37(10), 46–54 (2004)
3. Dey, A.: Providing Architectural Support for Building Context-Aware Applications, PhD thesis, College of Computing, Georgia Institute of Technology (December 2000)
4. Han, S., Nijdam, N., Schmid, J., Kim, J., Magnenat-Thalmann, N.: Collaborative telemedicine for interactive multiuser segmentation of volumetric medical images. The Visual Computer Journal 26, 639–648 (2010)

5. Keremitsis, E., Fuller, I.: HP Distributed Smalltalk: A Tool for Developing Distributed Applications. Hewlett-Packard Journal, 85–92 (1995)
6. Marsic, I.: An architecture for heterogeneous groupware applications. In: Proceedings of the 23rd International Conference on Software Engineering, pp. 475–484 (2001)
7. Roman, M., Hess, C., Cerqueira, R., Ranganathan, A., Campbell, R., Nahrstedt, K., Gaia: A Middleware Infrastructure to Enable Active Spaces. IEEE Pervasive Computing Magazine 1(4), 74–83 (2002)
8. Talukder, A., Yavagal, R.: Mobile Computing: Technology, Applications, and Service Creation. McGraw-Hill Professional (2006)
9. Ulmer, B., Ishii, H.: Emerging Frameworks for Tangible User Interfaces. IBM Systems Journal 39(3/4) (2000)
10. Weiser, M.: The Computer for the 21 Century. Scientific American 265, 94–101 (1991)

User Evaluation of Dynamic User-Centric Networking*

Raffaele Bolla[1], Riccardo Rapuzzi[1], and Matteo Repetto[2]

[1] Department of Communications, Computer and System Sciences (DIST),
University of Genoa, Via Opera Pia 13, 16145 Genoa, Italy
{raffaele.bolla,riccardo.rapuzzi}@unige.it
[2] Consorzio Nazionale Interuniversitario per le Telecomunicazioni (CNIT),
Viale G.P. Usberti 181/A, 43124 Parma, Italy
matteo.repetto@cnit.it

Abstract. In user-centric networking users become the endpoint of their communication sessions. This approach intrinsically accounts for mobility management, as terminal handovers and session migrations are expected when the user moves. However, effectiveness of session migration procedure is not trivial to assess, because it mainly concerns the subjective impressions that human users have about their interaction with the system, thus a common approach is to carry out user-evaluation at live demos.

In this paper we describe the user evaluation of our dynamic user-centric networking framework, done at a national science exhibition through a Voice-over-IP application running on top of it.

Keywords: User-centric networking, Mobility management, User-evaluation.

1 Introduction

Recently, the user-centric paradigm was applied to networking [1], by making users the endpoints of their multimedia sessions, whereas devices in their surrounding only are instruments to access networks and to interface with multimedia tools. In this approach, users are assigned a personal network identifier (i.e., the *Personal Address*, PA) for each of their communication sessions. Technically, that address is indeed bound to the device currently used, which performs network operations on behalf of the user.

Mobility management becomes integral part of the whole framework, in order to let users using any device and accessing any network in a seamless, transparent and automatic way. The current implementation of this framework exploits the Mobile IP (MIP) [2] infrastructure, which allows to deal with terminal handover and session migration in a uniform way (see [1] for details). Indeed, MIP only

---

* This work was partially funded by the EU 6th framework program, contract no. 38419 (Intermedia NoE).

F. Alvarez and C. Costa (Eds.): UCMEDIA 2010, LNICST 60, pp. 150–159, 2012.

deals with terminal mobility, but the powerful of the PA approach resides in realizing session migration as well on the same infrastructure.

Terminal handover with MIP has been thoroughly investigated in the past; however, session migration is a more recent application and its performance is not so much clear [1], [3], [4]. Preliminary measurements have already been carried out for the Personal Address framework, both in local environment and in Internet testbeds [1]; however, these results usually are difficult to interpret as effectiveness of session migration mainly concerns the subjective impressions humans have about their interaction with the system: just consider that the terminals often are not side by side, and the person may need several seconds to move to the new device.

This paper extends our previous work [1] with qualitative user evaluation of session migration in the PA framework: a live demo with a sample multimedia application was shown at an Italian national exhibition named "Festival of Science", where a large number of visitors got their feedback through compilation of questionnaires and direct interviews. The demo planning, the questionnaires and their analysis were organized with the support of a psychologist, who was already skilled in user evaluation for multimedia applications.

The paper is organized as follows: Section 2 describes the live demo and the application, Section 3 explains the procedure for evaluation and Section 4 analyzes the feedback and answers from visitors. Finally, we give our conclusions in Section 5, together with our plans for next developing.

2   The Live Demo

The networking framework was evaluated at the live demo through a very simple and minimal Voice-over-IP (VoIP) application based on the SIP protocol [5] for communication. Figure 1 shows the architectural elements for automatic session migration.

Mobility relies on the user-centric Personal Address framework described in [1]; the user identification (Chloe's PA in the picture) remains the same independently of the current device. The framework integrates with the SIP infrastructure; SIP extensions to handle session migration were already described in [1].

Sensor networks are in charge of locating the user. Sensors are MicaZ[1] motes, which operate at the 2.4 GHz ISM frequency band and adopt the IEEE 802.15.4 communication protocol [6]. Fixed sensors (anchors) are scattered in the environment, while one mote is worn by the user; the Context Server accumulates RSSI measurements from motes, estimates the user position and decides the most suitable device (that one closest to the user). Moreover, the Context Server is in charge of tracking the user position; the SIP proxy subscribes a localization service at the Context Server which notifies the current (closest) device every time the user moves.

---

[1] Crossbow Technologies, MicaZ Specification, http://www.xbow.com

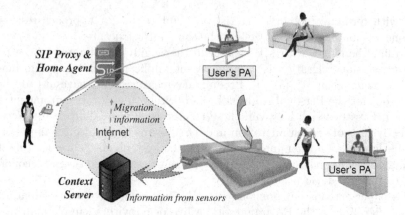

Fig. 1. Automatic session migration for interactive multimedia sessions

The VoIP client has a very minimal interface; it mainly provides buttons to start/stop the call, a few options (codecs, address book) and two rendering boxes: the largest displays the video of the remote user, and the smallest plays the video of the local user.

3 User Evaluation

We showed the live demo at the 2009 edition of the Festival of Science[2], Future Internet session. The Festival is held in Genoa and last year it was attended by 200,000 visitors from October 23rd to November 1st: 160,000 people visited exhibitions and laboratories whilst 40,000 people attended conferences, shows and free-access events. They were professionals and skilled people, young students, science fans and mere curious people. We stayed at the Festival two days (October 23rd – 24th) and got feedback from 101 users.

Visitors tried the demo themselves after a short introduction about the Intermedia project[3] and the meaning of automatic session migration.

Three laptops were deployed as user terminals; two of them were assigned to the mobile user, whilst the third was used by the correspondent user. Two sensors were lying near each terminal and one anchor sensor was tied to the wrist of the mobile user by a strip of velcro (see Fig. 2(a)).

One user started the VoIP call and the other answered. Then, the "mobile" was asked to move to and fro between his terminals (see Fig. 2(b)), so he could evaluate the responsiveness of the automatic session migration (there was no way to separate localization and session migration); the corresponding user saw a freezing image during the migration and could assess the nuisance value of this interruption.

---

[2] Festival della Scienza, http://www.festivalscienza.it In Italian.
[3] The InterMedia project, URL: http://intermedia.miralab.ch/

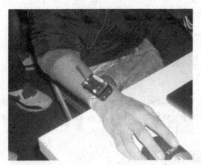

(a) The sensor tied to the user's wrist.

(b) The user moves during the demo.

Fig. 2. Screenshots from the live demo

After they had tried the demo, users were asked to compile the question-naire. The assessment phase was not limited to that issue; indeed, it was also extended to the previous two phases by observing commonly asked questions from users, their difficulties while using the migration service, their comments and suggestions for improvement.

The questionnaire was organized in three parts concerning user profiles (age, gender, education, work, familiarity with and use of technologies in daily life), assessment of the live demo (usability and responsiveness), suggestions and im-provements.

4   Analysis of Results

4.1   Users Profile

The questionnaire was filled in by 101 people (48 females, 53 males), aged be-tween 10–69. In the analysis of results we divided the subjects based on their age, as shown in Table 1.

Most people who completed the questionnaire are schools, high schools and university students (69 people). The other part of the sample is rather hetero-geneous in terms of education and employment; they are teachers, employees, professional men, housewives, unemployed people and pensioners with a school-leaving certificate or a university degree.

Most of the sample feels skilled with technology and uses several devices every day (see Table 2) . They usually use 7 devices on average out of 12 we suggested them, mainly televisions (98%), mobile phones (97%) and PCs (86%).

4.2   Evaluation of the Test Session

The first question was the effort in understanding the migration feature (im-mediateness of use), which only means the level of difficulty in learning how to

Table 1. Number of questionnaires for different age groups

Age	<14	15-19	20-29	30-50	>50
# users	25	36	15	13	12

Table 2. Number of used devices proposed in the questionnaire and familiarity with technology. Evaluation of familiarity with technology is placed on a Likert scale from 1 up to 5, where 5 indicates a great familiarity and 1 no familiarity.

	Mean	SD	Min	Max
# devices	7.35	2.07	1	11
Familiarity	3.92	0.74	·2	5

use the migration service. The second question concerned how quick the migration had happened (speed). The following questions were about the usefulness of session migration among multimedia devices: how much users liked this feature (pleasant), their assessment about its usefulness in everyday life (utility) and how much they would spend to use it (value). The assessment of the economic value of the feature was proposed in Euros according to the following arbitrary scale: above 20 (5); 5 up to 20 (4); less than 5 (3); nothing, I would only use it whether it were free (2); nothing, I would not use it (1). Mean values for each age class are shown in Table 3.

Table 3. User feeling about the migration feature for each age range. Users answered these questions on a Likert scale from 1 to 5, where 5 is the more positive and 1 is the more negative opinion.

	Immediateness	Speed	Pleasant	Utility	Value
<14	4.16	4.24	4.76	4.48	4.12
15-19	3.94	4.14	4.22	3.89	3.97
20-29	4.13	4.21	4.50	4.00	3.31
30-50	3.92	4.08	4.46	4.00	3.42
> 50	3.92	4.08	4.75	4.08	4.08

As the results show, the effort to understand the user interface and the migration feature was acceptable; further, we may note younger generations required less effort, as probably they are friendlier and more used to modern technologies than eldest people. The rapidity of migration mainly depends on the Personal Address and the mobility framework, as the delay introduced by media codec in video acquisition and rendering is almost negligible; we got a good score here, thus we can take the quantitative analysis for the local testbed given in [1] as a good benchmark for assessing the effectiveness of session migration.

The second part of the evaluation shows a substantial interest by users towards the demo scenario and their willingness to accept the migration feature in the next future; this feedback motivates our work and future research in this field. Users like the feature to migrate an interactive video session among devices, they consider the service useful and they would spend some money for it. A MANOVA [7] analysis has been conducted to check if there were differences in the answers by different age groups; no relevant variation has arisen among those groups in assessing usability and suitability of the migration service to the needs and interests of potential users. Finally, innovation has been evaluated by asking users whether they had ever found session migration in any application. Most people (86% of interviewed) considered the migration service innovative, as they had never seen before this functionality. A small percentage (9%) said they had already seen similar application, but oral interviews following the compilation of the questionnaires pointed out that most of them refer to side aspects of the demo, which are not related with session migration, as the use of webcam and VoIP calls. Finally, few users (about 3%) found the migration service similar to other kinds of functionality: the GPS localization available in the iPhone, the automatic re-tuning to a different frequency providing the same station when the first signal becomes too weak (e.g., when moving out of range) usually found in car stereo systems (AF function of the RDS[4] system), the handover mechanism of cellular networks.

4.3 Indication from Users

The last part of the questionnaire investigates how users perceive our technology and their feeling with related ethical issues; in particular, we are interested in understanding whether they found the migration framework intrusive, whether they are afraid of their privacy to be violated and which kind of devices they would be willing to interact with.

As an indication for future investigation, we asked users what applications they expect the feature to be available for. Indeed, our demo falls into the most rated application: phone calls (74%), watching TV (53%), listen to music (49%), Internet browsing (40%), videogames (38%), chat (34%), work (23%), and other (2%). Figure 3 shows the preferred user applications for each age group; in this case there are significant differences. For example, 80% of users aged under 14 would like to use the migration service to play videogames, whilst the corresponding percentage for the other groups is significantly lower (range 15-19 = 31%, range 20-29 = 33%, range 30-50 = 0%, > 50= 17%). Note that the youngest people always have higher percentage than other groups; this means they checked off a larger number of items for this question; the only exception is the work item, as users under 14 are students and are not involved with such activity.

From a technological point of view, users expect the migration feature on most of their daily equipment: televisions (83%), cell phones (71%), PCs (67%), laptops (51%), MP3 players (33%), stereos (26%), fixed phone (24%), DVD players (23%), PDAs (20%), smart phones (19%), car stereos (17%) and others

---

[4] Radio Data System, http://www.rds.org.uk/

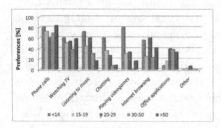

Fig. 3. Preferred applications for session migration

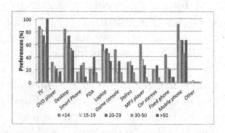

Fig. 4. Preferred devices for session migration

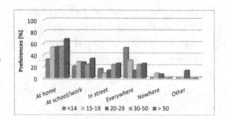

Fig. 5. Where users wish the migration function be available

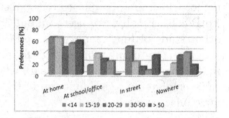

Fig. 6. Where users are willing to be located

(1%). This implies the algorithm must be kept simple enough to be ported on a wide range of different devices. The preferred devices vary with age (see Figure 4): 100% of the oldest users (> 50) checked off television, while 92% of youngest people (under 14) selected the cell phone. Other devices voted by a large number of people are desktops and laptops.

Session migration is a component of pervasive communication; however, users may not need pervasive communication everywhere. Indeed, user feedback has been quite surprising for us: they mainly expect session migration at home (which is the preferred answer of eldest people), and only in lower percentage everywhere (which is the preferred answer of youngest users). Figure 5 shows the detailed answers for each age group.

As a side effect of automatic session migration, users movements have to be tracked and this may concern privacy issue for many people. Taking into account the behavior according to age, all groups agree that home is a perfect place to locate sensors, while disagree in the other responses (see Figure 6): perhaps people believe a tracking system working in home environment keeps all data on private equipment and does not allow anybody to access such information. People who did not like to be located anywhere knew cellular systems indeed maintain information about the cell of their phone; we have argued people are willing to postpone their qualms about privacy whether they are really interested in the service.

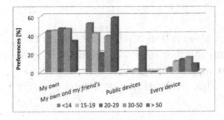

Fig. 7. Which devices people would migrate their sessions to

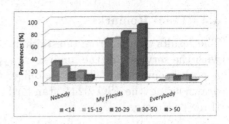

Fig. 8. Willingness of users to share their personal devices with other people

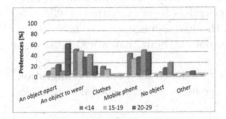

Fig. 9. Users preference about the placement of the sensor they have to bring with them

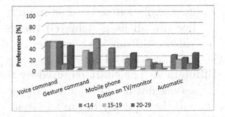

Fig. 10. Users preferences about control of session migration

People aged 15-19 have a higher percentage at school/office than other group. This last fact is quite curious as well, as teenagers often care about let their parents know they are (or are not) at school!

Another issue in pervasive communication is the presence of public, shared and private devices in the environment. Most people would use their own devices and those of their friends, but few users are interested in third parties' and public devices (Figure 7). Indeed, this group includes university students and young workers which are usually more used to share computers and other devices with their colleagues.

The other side of the problem concerns sharing of users devices. The result is congruent with the previous question: people are not inclined to share devices with third parties (Figure 8), yet older users are more willing to share their devices with people they know.

Coming back to more technical issue, sensors may be integrated in several objects users usually bring with them, and the main question here is what kind of object the users would like. Many differences arise among answers from the different groups (see Figure 9). Users who chose an object to wear or other specified that it could be a clock.

Finally, we cared about the control of session migration. The automatic feature was appreciated by many users, but they also like other forms of control (see Figure 10). Also in this case, there are many differences among the different age groups.

4.4   Final Remarks

The results coming from questionnaires, the observation of the user interaction with the service and the analysis of type and number of errors allow us to give a positive judgment about usability of the migration service (conclusions are drawn using the ISO 9241 standard [8]). This evaluation takes into account three parameters:

Effectiveness. The level of achievement of the objectives. The first and simplest effectiveness index is the achievement of the objective: a product is effective if it carries out its task. Otherwise, if the objective is not achieved, the effectiveness can be measured in terms of number of operations towards its completion state. The migration service has been evaluated as effective because all users achieved the goal in the live demo, i.e. they migrated a video call from one computer to another one, without they were required to take any control action.

Efficiency. The effort required by the user to achieve the goal. The migration service has been evaluated efficient because users easily learned how it works and they quickly began to use it.

User Satisfaction. The perceived usefulness of the service by users. The service was evaluated useful by users and they talked positively about the migration concept.

More feedbacks were collected by analyzing answers, comments and critics from the users during the demo. This information provides us useful indications about aspects that should be taken into account in following developments. For example:

- **Security:** Users were interested in security and privacy issues involved in using devices owned by other people.
- **Human-Machine Interface (HMI):** Many users, especially the youngest, underlined the importance of improving the service interface and physical aspect of sensors; obviously these are minor remarks for our purposes, as our framework works at the network layer and the VoIP application was only developed to set up a live demo, while at the current stage sensors are only prototypes and are far from a real product. About control of migration, a clear and unique trend does not appear from users; indeed, answers from users suggest that different solutions could be integrated, according to different user profiles and preferences.

Finally, the last remarkable aspect to be considered was the tendency of adult users to perceive the migration service as a futuristic technology, while younger users seemed more inclined to use this technology in daily life straightaway.

5   Conclusions

This paper reports our experience and user evaluation we did in a live demo. Users appreciated the performance of our user-centric framework and were interested in its implementation in daily applications and commonly used devices.

The Personal Address framework currently exploits the MIP framework, which is known leading to poor performance and resource wasting. Nevertheless, the feedback we got was very positive: users declared themselves satisfied in terms of migration speed; indeed, we must remark the drawbacks of MIP are less evident in local scenarios.

The live demo demonstrated the feasibility of bringing the user-centric paradigm to networking as well; our future work will progress towards two main directions. On the one hand, we will investigate more powerful and efficient overlay architectures to manage the Personal Address and mobility issues. On the other hand, we will study new architectural paradigms for the Future Internet, where both users and content are natively the session endpoints and can be addressed directly (without any overlay infrastructure) at the network layer.

Acknowledgements. The authors would like to thanks Stefano Chessa and his staff at ISTI-CNR in Pisa for their invaluable help in providing the localization by sensor networks framework used in the live demo.

The authors would also thanks Ludovica Primavera who assisted them in preparing the questionnaires, interviewing visitors during the live demo and carrying out user evaluation in a professional and qualified way.

References

1. Bolla, R., Rapuzzi, R., Repetto, M.: An integrated mobility framework for pervasive communications. In: IEEE Global Communications Conference (IEEE Globecom 2009), Honolulu, Hawaii, USA (2009)
2. Perkins, C.: IP mobility support for IPv4. RFC 3344 (2002)
3. Lu, W., Lo, A., Niemegeers, I.: Session mobility support for personal networks using Mobile IPv6 and VNAT. In: 5th Workshop on Applications and Services in Wireless Networks (ASWN 2005), Paris, France (2005)
4. Kohn, R.: Delegated IP: A Mobile IPv6-based protocol to support session delegation. In: IEEE International Conference on Communications (ICC 2008), pp. 3279–3285 (2008)
5. Rosemberg, J., Schulzrinne, H., Camarillo, G., Johnston, A., Sparks, R., Handley, A., Schooler, E.: SIP: Session Initiation Protocol. RFC 3261 (2002)
6. Bolla, R., Rapuzzi, R., Repetto, M., Barsocchi, P., Chessa, S., Lenzi, S.: Automatic multimedia session migration by means of a context-aware mobility framework. In: The International Conference for Mobility Technology, Applications and Systems (ACM Mobility Conference 2009), Nice, France (2009)
7. Stevens, J.P.: Applied multivariate statistics for the social sciences, Lawrence Erblaum, Mahwah, NJ (2002)
8. ISO 9241-11:1998: Ergonomic requirements for office work with visual display terminals (VDTs) – part 11: Guidance on usability (1998)

Author Index